M000030967

EXCELLENCE
IN MUSIC MINISTRY

Word of Faith Family Church
woffc.tv
YouTube-Facebook

EXCELLENCE
IN MUSIC MINISTRY

An Inward Foundation For An Outward Expression

Steven James Ingram

Scripture quotations marked KJV are taken from *The Holy Bible, King James Version*. Scripture quotations marked AMP are taken from *The Amplified® Bible* , Copyright © 1954, 1958, 1962, 1964, 1987 by The Lockman Foundation. Used by permission. (www.Lockman.org) Scripture quotations marked THE MESSAGE are taken from *The Message*, Copyright © 1993, 1994, 1995, 1996, 2000, 2001, 2002. Used by permission of NavPress Publishing Group. Emphasis within Scripture is the author's own. Please note that IMI's publishing style capitalizes certain pronouns in Scripture that refer to the Father, Son, and Holy Spirit and may differ from some Bible publishers' styles. Take note that the name satan and related names are not capitalized. We choose not to acknowledge him, even to the point of violating grammatical rules.

Readers should be aware that Internet Web sites offered as citations and/or sources for further information may have changed or disappeared between the time this was written and when it is read.

Excellence in Music Ministry
ISBN: 978-1-936750-76-4
Copyright © 2011 by Steven James Ingram

Cover Art by Mark Herron © 1990

Published by IMI Publishing
PO Box 160220
Altamonte Springs, Fl 32716

407-834-0077

Printed in the United States of America. All rights reserved under International Copyright Law. No part of this publication may be reproduced, stored in a retrieval system or transmitted to any form or by any means—electronic, mechanical, photocopying, recording, or otherwise—without prior written consent of the Author.

ENDORSEMENTS

There are many gifted musicians, singers, and artists in our world today. I would venture to say that the greatest missing link in the life of any musician, singer, or artist is a genuine understanding of why their gift even exists—let alone how to use it. It is safe to say that music or sound is the single greatest weapon of either light or darkness in our world. It literally sets the stage for every natural occurrence whether good or bad.

The very sound we allow to penetrate our atmosphere establishes the way we think, feel and live our daily life. It is as critical to living as the air we breathe. It is sad that so few understand its true purpose either in heaven or earth. Ingrained in the very core of a sound is its ability to carry spiritual power. It will carry either light or darkness… either God's spirit or a spirit of darkness.

The very day anyone discovers the power of a sound and its ultimate purpose under heaven is the day he or she becomes dangerous to darkness and a powerful force for God in this world. If you are a musician, singer or artist, on that day you will break free from all the bondage and damage that living under the lies of a "star" or "popularity" driven life can bring.

Steve, I applaud you for being brave and sensitive enough to tell it like it is…for being a force to raise the bar for anyone who will read your words. *Excellence In Music Ministry* should be a must in the curriculum of anyone serious about pursuing their gift and calling before God. Really, if "caught," it will change the life of any musician or singer who takes the time to read its words.

Phil Driscoll
Grammy award winning singer/trumpeter/psalmist

In his book, *Excellence In Music Ministry*, Steve Ingram brilliantly shares his 30 years of experience developing a ministry of excellence. This is valuable teaching that every worship leader, worship team and musician should know in order to build on a solid foundation of excellence. It's a "must read" for leaders!

Martha Munizzi
Stellar award winning contemporary gospel artist

Excellence in Music Ministry is a very timely and much needed book for worship leaders and pastors. The author is saying a lot of the things that many of us have thought and prayed about for many years! This one will become a textbook in our worship classes. Thanks Pastor Steve for all the hard work and long hours. The spirit of excellence is evident in every chapter! Highly Recommended!!!

Morris Chapman
Songwriter/recording artist,
known as the "grandfather" of
contemporary praise and worship music

I have known Steve for over 30 years and have had the joy of sitting under his ministry of music and experiencing the anointing which brings the presence of God. His new book, *Excellence In Music Ministry*, is a work that reflects the scope of his experience in music and the development of his passion for worshipping God and training His Church to do the same.

This book is a must read for every music minister and every person endeavoring to use their God-given gift of music for the work of the ministry with the purpose of exalting and worshipping God. Steve stresses the importance of a strong, foundational relationship with God along with the on-going call for spiritual growth and development. He speaks of having a true hunger for God and being led by the Spirit as the most vital elements for allowing the creation of music.

The passion for music must go hand-in-hand with commitment to the church and its leadership, and serving where you are called, knowing that walking in holiness coincides with building character and developing musical technique.

Jerry Savelle
Internationally known minister,
author, teacher and television host

What is worship? It is more than sight and sound. It is light. Through worship, we see the light of God and light for our lives. This is one of the fresh insights Dr. Steve Ingram, shares in his new book, *Excellence In Music Ministry*. Whatever God has called you to do, be a writer, musician, worship leader, arranger, director or all of this and more, the truths and teachings of this book will propel you and your ministry forward and ignite renewed passion for God and His worship. Music inspires, excites, comforts and communicates. Anointed and skillful music changes the world and the worshipper! What has God called you to do? Let this faithful man of God teach you and take you to a new level.

Angela Courte
Host of the *Power of Praise*
nationally syndicated television show

Dr. Steve Ingram has a literal "Fort Knox" of experience as worship leader, pastor, music director, arranger, and master musician. Here, in one book, is a treasure trove of revelation, information and direction distilled from a life fully dedicated to worshipping God and equipping Christians.

Rare, indeed, is a work that includes such perfectly targeted subject matter and proven principles. This book is a "must read" for every worship leader, pastor and church member. *Excellence in Music Ministry* will, without doubt, become a textbook and success manual for all who embrace His presence.

Len Mink
Len Mink Ministries
Worship leader for Kenneth Copeland Ministries

Steve Ingram has had a lifetime of ministry excellence. This book gives credible insights into the how-to's, purpose and outcome of excellence in ministry. This is a must read for all worship leaders and team members.

Steve Bowersox
Bowersox Institute of Music

I can personally attest that Steve and Cheryl Ingram are world class musicians and psalmists. But more importantly they are Heaven class worshipers who are first and foremost passionate performers for the "audience of one," our Heavenly Father. Through their many years of educating and mentoring leaders and musicians of true worship, they have proven that they understand, and can communicate the Biblical principles that produce real fruit in the lives of their students.

These principles are wonderfully displayed in Dr. Steve Ingram's book, *Excellence In Music Ministry.*

This book is truly a "must read" for any worship leader, minister of music, musician, singer, choir member, or anyone who desires to engage and please the Lord with their worship. Dr. Ingram's sensitivity to the challenges that face today's Christian musicians and singers is countered with strong meat Biblical instruction, seasoned and served up with humor and great integrity, and is just the balanced, pastoral, approach that you would expect from such a true man of God.

I had the opportunity to work with Steve and Cheryl Ingram when I played drums for their music group Alpenglow way back in the ancient days of the mid-seventies. My admiration for them and their ministry began back then and has increased continually as I have watched their ministry mature and flourish. I am proud to call them my friends.

Dr. Steve Ingram received a Doctor of Sacred Music degree from Life Christian University in 1997, and is one or the most distinguished and deserving music ministers to have ever received this degree.

Dr. Douglas J. Wingate
President and Founder, Life Christian University

CONTENTS

FOREWORD

I look back 50 years to the time I accepted Jesus as my Savior. I had been a singer of songs since I was a child. Who taught me, my music teacher? No—the radio.

As I grew older I learned to "sell" the song. I was a song salesman. If I was to get paid for what I did, someone had to buy my product. When I sang in clubs or on stage, I was selling two products—the song and myself. If the song was weak, I had to work harder to sell it. Some songs just didn't sell at all. Nobody wanted to hear them. So what now? Write something they want to hear—something sad, lonely or blue.

Then when I began singing to people in church all I knew to do was sell the song and me. I could tell there was something wrong with that, but I was so ignorant of the Word and God's way of doing things, I couldn't tell what it was. Once I was thrust into the Word of Faith and the reality of the Kingdom of God, I realized I was no longer a song salesman. I am a preacher of the Word. Period! In season or out! In song or out! Preach THE WORD.

It's the anointing that removes burdens and destroys yokes. Removing burdens and destroying yokes is the bottom line, not performing, not building a ministry, or raising money, or any of the other things that go along with "gospel" stuff. I took a lot of time falling flat on my face in the middle of a song when the anointing would just fly away like a bird and leave me standing there feeling stark naked. I stopped. I didn't finish the song. I said, "That's enough of that." When I began preaching the Word, the anointing returned. That's when I began seeking the truth about that part of my calling.

Oh, how I would have been thrilled with a book like *Excellence in Music Ministry* written by someone with not only the obvious God-given ability, but also the Word knowledge to go along with it. To be able to study after a ministry of excellence that has been proven in time and by fire is truly an honor and privilege.

Read it. Pray it. Study it! Steve's book? No. The Word of God! Use Steve's book and his example of life and ministry as a help and guide to the abundant life and ministry Jesus has provided for those who will do it His way. His way works.

Jesus is Lord!

Kenneth Copeland

Kenneth Copeland

ACKNOWLEGEMENTS

With humbleness of heart and with great gratitude, I would like to acknowledge the various men and women of God who have strategically influenced my life and thus the pages of this book. Some may have no idea of their influence, while others have had a more direct and personable attribute to the place I am today. Regardless, I deem it honorable to thank them publically. Some have entered Heaven already without hearing my gratitude, but I gladly pronounce my thankfulness and called them blessed. Without intention, there are many who have influenced me that I have momentarily probably overlooked, but nonetheless, I'm so very thankful.

First, to the Father God, Elder Brother Jesus, The Holy Spirit and all of the Heavenly Hosts, thank YOU for your patience as I have slowly gained focus concerning my destiny. We will enjoy many, many more measures of heart sounds together.

To my Dad and Mom, Daniel Armstead Ingram and Clyde Lovett Ingram, I cannot say enough for the joy of growing up in a Godly, joy filled home where my gifting and pursuit of music was first endured and then later enjoyed…I think. Your personal financial sacrifices purchased that first Wurlitzer Spinet and the lessons I took twice a week. I am eternally grateful.

To the many generous, patient, piano and music teachers who gave polite approval and encouragement when I was unprepared or tried to fudge by using my ear ability to pretend to play… Thank you! You were never fooled. Mrs. A.A. Davis, my first piano teacher who taught me to value the written note and would rap my knuckles with a pencil when I used the wrong fingering. Thank you Kathy Nelson, Mrs. Nosco and Florida State Professor, Mr. John Boda, Mrs. Murphy, Dr. Maurice King and so many more for hours and hours of patience with my inaccurate scales, fingering and reading. Though you were paid to teach my fingers, you all gave so much more. Thank you!

I give a very special thanks to Ken and Kathy Nelson for giving me a job in their music store, Nelson Music, where I learned so much about the inner workings and facets of pianos and the business that surrounds it. Ms. Kathy provided a much needed firm, loving, and instruction into excellence of music ministry. She got me on a wonderful musical path, and today I'm so grateful. Thank you both so much.

To the many pastors and choir directors who also patiently, lovingly, gave of themselves and their ministries to allow me to be a team player, I'm very appreciative.

I pause also to thank the many, many other, clinicians, mentors, and musicians—singers that I've played a few measures of music with. Thank you to all of these and so many more that I've drawn inspiration from. From the School of the Psalmist™ times… David Wright, Art Osborne, Keith Jourdan, Chris and Carole Beatty, Dr. Steve Bowersox, Dr. Rick Powell, Dr. James Burgdorf and David VanKoevering. To various studio musicians and singers; Leonard Jones, Dennis Holt, Pat Bryan, Ira Watson, Janny Grein, Mike Deasy, Stan Nixon, Dave Smith, Durant Beasley, Len Mink, Abraham Laboriel, Harlan Rogers, Bill Maxwell, Alex Acuna, Ben Tankard- thank you. To various teachers; Dr. Jack Hayford, Dr. Myles Munroe, Dr. Creflo Dollar, Dr. Hilton Sutton, Dr. Jerry Savelle, Ron Kenoly, Judson Cornwall, Robert Webber, George and Terri Pearsons (our pastors) C.S. Lewis, J.S. Bach, PDQ Bach, Ralph Carmichael, John Williams, Russ Ferrante (Yellow-Jackets) Dave Grusin, Henry Mancini and so many more. Thank you all.

I give a very sincere thank you to the hundreds of IMI School of Ministry and Music students who attended and graduated around the world. Your ears were patience and your acceptance smiles stirred me, as I shared over and over many of these principles.

With that said I'm also indebted to all the Covenant members and partners of Word of Faith Family Church in Daytona Beach. I am very appreciative of our wonderful staff led by IMI graduates Andrew and

Liebe Mowbray, Administrative Pastors of Word of Faith. These two have worked tirelessly, without fanfare, or recognition.

Thank you especially Kenneth and Gloria Copeland, who graciously added me to their crusade team in 1979 as a pianist. During my twelve years of participation in traveling, writing and arranging songs, studio productions, and the many other efforts since, your impeccable, accurate, Bible teachings and encouragement have become a large part of my thinking process today. Your spirit of excellence of the Word and ministry has had the single most impact to my pursuit of the Father and Worship. The day I learned from you to apply the force of faith on the notes that I played, I saw and have experienced a different level of anointing ever since. Learning to apply my faith changed my way of everything. Early on, you taught me the value of making a quality decision from which there is no retreat. Brother Ken, your pursuit of excellence in your own powerful psalmist ministry has always stirred my heart to press for more and more. I am blessed by your love for the song of the Lord when many today have little respect or knowledge of its value. Thank you, Kenneth and Gloria, for such a consistent, unwavering ministry of excellence.

I must also thank Phil Driscoll who I first met in his BC (before Christ) days, circa 1976. I have always been blessed by your anointed, skillful ministry and more over your numerous personal insights about light and the releasing of Heavenly sound. From the early days of echo-plex and midi, to the high tech digital wireless tools of today and beyond, you're always on the leading forefront. I know of no other vessel alive today who understands, demonstrates, and ministers musically in that Heavenly realm as you do, Phil. Thank you for so many years of generous impartation and encouraging friendship.

I leave the last thank you and acknowledgement for the two most important people in my life—my wife Cheryl, best friend, lover, singer, song writer, psalmist, and partner in ministry, and Mr. Steve Jr. our only son, and best encourager of a Dad ever! He is an excellent writer, musician, eternal optimist, "sonmeister," and has a wonderful sense of joy about his calling. Thank you so!

INTRODUCTION

Godly living brings such wonderful people and ideas into your existence. As a young man, I had no clue what the adult part of my life would be. I was raised in South Georgia where most kids went off to college, typically the University of Georgia, and then would come home to marry their high school sweetheart. As wonderful a plan as it may be, that's not what happened, or should I say, that's not what was designed for me.

After high school graduation, I went off to Florida State University in Tallahassee, Florida, only a few miles from my home in Bainbridge, Georgia, where I proceeded to grow in musical ability, playing piano anywhere I could. Most of my time was occupied by playing in bands, recitals, and clubs, accompanying other students, and in holding many church pianist and organist positions. I loved the environment of being a music student. Sadly, I discovered that you have to go other classes as well. English, History and Trigonometry subjects just didn't seem to capture my attention as being all that necessary. A year and half later, I was invited to leave that wonderful institution, and it was suggested that I attend a small junior community college in Madison, Florida. After a somewhat slow season of maturing, finally graduating from the junior college, and then enrolling at Valdosta State College to finish my music education degree, something radical happened to me. On the road to hell…I got saved…you know…born again!

Within a few months, I had dropped out of college and began pursuing the use of music in communicating this wonderful Gospel that had so drastically changed my life. Two college buddies, Steve Appel,

Dave Guthrie, and I decided to open a Christian coffeehouse called Aunt Helens Store. The "store" was a venue where we served coffee and other refreshments and where kids mostly gathered for conversation. I didn't initially envision a Christian club, but rather a communication center with all avenues of entertainment combined. A wonderful local couple, Pastor Walter Edwards and his wife, Iris, of the First United Methodist Church, who were radical themselves with the love of God, aided and guided our efforts. The Edwards had a wonderful world view about the Kingdom of God and helped to solidify my thinking in so many ways. It was also via their love for God that my theology base began to widen and grow as they introduced me to the writings of C.S. Lewis, Dietrich Bonhoeffer and others. Captions such as "discipleship," "witness," and "conversational evangelism" became our topics.

The name Aunt Helen's Store actually came from the tag on the front door key given to us of the same defunct downtown Madison business storefront. We were given the opportunity to use that abandoned storefront to house a place for local college kids to hang out while we used our talents, and somewhat immature spirituality, to see students' lives changed. Eclectic music, poetry readings, skits, old black and white Charlie Chaplin movies, and other forms of musical entertainment, which would have certainly been frowned upon in most of the nominal churches, were standard fare at Aunt Helen's Store. We would perform our versions of Simon and Garfunkle, the Beatles and off the wall poetry. We also performed the new Christian musical, *Good News*.[1] All of it communicated the love of God in a contemporary style, at least in our ears and from our hearts.

It was that modest evangelistic effort that brought attention from a street ministry in Miami, Florida called Surfside Challenge. A mutual local musician friend brought the director to meet me. Surfside Challenge was a drug rehabilitation interdiction center, which specialized in housing drug addicts and troubled youth for a six to nine month period. This aggressive, nonconventional, street ministry wanted me to duplicate my expertise for their inner-city outreach in Miami. After one visit to

---

[1] ©1967, Billy Ray Hearn, "Good News," Broadman Press

Miami, and seeing the drastic need and immense potential presented, I decided to accept their offer. I did not know that God was setting me up! To the dismay of my parents and friends, I left the work at Aunt Helen's Store in Madison, and moved further south to Miami, the testing ground and practical laboratory of my faith—walk—life in Jesus Christ. Again, Heaven had plans for me that I knew nothing about!

After scouting various areas of this Ephesus—like metropolis, we settled on Coconut Grove, a hippie type, bohemian—styled community, nestled in the midst of expensive high rises, sailboats in Key Biscayne, a local playhouse, and many storefront head shops. The area was where drug paraphernalia, occult book stores, and many tie dyed bell bottom stores were all readily available. We created a place called The Parable Coffeehouse on Grand Avenue adjacent to a ghetto area. We wanted to minister life to ALL. We did.

Several times a day and in the evenings, we would serve free food and music combined with a lot of loving conversations about God. I had become convinced by this time that I was going to be a lifelong "musicionary," a missions minded musician, utilizing my skills and love for people as my career. More and more the idea of marriage, a wife or a typical family life was disappearing from my thoughts in lieu of honoring God with my gift and calling. God always has a better plan than we can dream.

In early spring of 1972, the leadership of the street ministry decided that we needed to go to various Christian colleges and solicit students for a summer campaign of witnessing. We appealed to a zealous college age group of volunteers for a short two month's mission effort unlike one they had ever experienced. To aid the introduction of the ministry to students, I put together a group of musicians. The band was developed from some of the now ex-drug kids of Surfside Challenge. It was certainly a diverse and unique group of rock and roll players. We embarked with great expectation and a sense of relief from the daily routine of Coconut Grove. We were able to see other parts of the country as well as meet new people.

It was in Cleveland, Tennessee at Lee College, now Lee University, that I encountered my future head on. The leader of Surfside Challenge had invited several students from the college to join us musically in one of the promotional rallies. One night before the rally, we met in the basement of a professor's home for a short rehearsal, which was the day my reality met my destiny. One of the students, Allyn Cheryl Bunch, walked down the basement stairs with her college roommate following behind. My eyes locked on her as she seemed to descend the stairs in slow motion. Cheryl and her roommate took out their guitars and proceeded to sing. I was suddenly startled and mesmerized. She was awesome, very beautiful, and though petite, her voice was so bold for such a small package of a woman. She was full of joy! I was smitten. Completing the rally, I didn't want to leave that college campus, but the Parable Coffeehouse was my assignment. I did not let my feelings for the petite young lady be known.

Later that summer, Cheryl, her roommate and singing partner, Daphne Swilling, and another friend took Surfside Challenge up on the offer to experience that once in a lifetime summer missions out-reach. They joined us in street ministry, passed out tracts, witnessed and sang nightly at the Parable Coffeehouse. While staff members were not allowed any romantic relationships in this ministry, inwardly I nonethe-less fell deeply in love with her and her gift for God! The bump in the road was that she wasn't so inclined…I later discovered.

When summer was ending and Fall Semester approached, the "girls," Cheryl and Daphne, made the decision to stay for a few more months in Miami. Street ministry is contagious. When you see lives changed day after day you become addicted to the prospect of one more addition to the family of God. They caught that vision and got permission from their parents to stay longer. One night in late 1972, after our staff duties with supper and securing that the students were in their rooms, I asked Cheryl to go with me for a short walk around our complex area. Imagine the ambiance of a full moon shining through the palm tree lined blocks of a beautiful Miami neighborhood. The air was pungent with the smell of Cuban coffee; however she had insisted that the "air" be cleared of an outrageous rumor. She had heard that I was in love with her and wanted a relationship. Yes, it was a "moon over Miami" Hallmark moment that was quickly becoming a tragic love story. We were not off to a good start here. She first declared her appreciation for me, but insisted on my understanding that she would be returning to college and certainly wasn't interested in me "in that way." She was thankful for our time and relationship musically, but there would be NO future for us beyond that!

God has a way to test your resolve, your metal, and He always requires a leap of faith for His involvement. So, there I was almost dying inside at hearing her pronouncement when suddenly I became BOLD! Not desperate but B-O-L-D! FORWARD!

As we walked down the sidewalk, I asked her to take a seat on a stucco fence that famously front some Miami yards. I suddenly heard myself say, "Well that may be true, Cheryl Bunch, but I know that when I first laid eyes on you in Tennessee as you came down those stairs at that rehearsal, my life was making a major turn, and I knew then that YOU would forever be in it! I love you...there I said it. I want to marry you...and I see nothing else. Now that I've said that... it's your problem. I love you." Silence... yes and then... more silence. But God...

I was looking for some kind of sign as I gazed up into the balmy Miami night sky. After a few moments, she opened her mouth and spoke words that changed the course of history for this South Georgia musician. Out of the silence Cheryl said, "Well, I love you too." She later conveyed to me that she didn't know where that remark came from. Her head was telling her she was crazy, but her heart was letting her know this was right. She didn't know how she would tell Daphne, since they had plans that didn't include Miami, Surfside Challenge and especially ME. Over the next several weeks we didn't date, but spent more time getting to know and understand what God had for us. We became engaged and were married on September 1, 1973 at Vizcaya Gardens and Museum in Coconut Grove, Miami Florida! Thank God for our lives together through which I've learned so much of what this worship lifestyle and book is about. My wife is a true worshipper and an awesome, anointed prophetic psalmist. I am eternally indebted to the grace and Love of God for including her in my life.

So it is to her, Allyn Cheryl Bunch Ingram that I dedicate with honor these pages and Godly information into your life. Without her input, her zeal for God, and certainly her spirit of excellence, you might be reading this information from some other author today. Investigate on your own and discover Cheryl's wonderfully passionate teachings and music projects.

Thank you, Cheryl, my sweetheart, wife, love and best friend for all your years of encouragement and support and for bringing our son, Steven James Ingram, Jr. into this world. What a delight he is. You, Junior and Jesus really know how to make me smile...

We should pause for a Hallmark Channel musical soundtrack...

CHAPTER ONE

PRELUDE FOR EXCELLENCE

The pursuit of excellence in every arena of life requires focus, discipline, and sacrifices. Success in regard to excellence is a never ending pursuit. However measured, it is not for the casual pursuer who feels as though they can get by without a disciplined heart. Excellence always requires a determined effort.

The boldness to declare a title such as, *Excellence in Music Ministry*, comes with several distinct qualifications. One must realize the object is not music ministry, but to become an unashamed vessel whose heart is chasing after God. Once these processes are completed and infused into your thinking and daily routine, there is the constant awareness that you've still not arrived. In other words, every disciplined student realizes that this becomes a lifestyle and not a destination. The Word underlines for us, "…we are constantly being transfigured into His very own image in ever increasing splendor and from one degree of glory to another; [*for this comes*] from the Lord [*Who is*] the Spirit." (2 Corinthians 3:18b AMP)

My effort and intent in these pages is to lay a plan that will entice and engage the novice student as well as encourage the seasoned believer into another fresh level of pursuit of Father God and His bestowed giftings. With each chapter, I am endeavoring to assist you in a new mindset of hunger for excellence in music ministry. In reality, excellence is a by-product of running your race with patience. Run this glorious life-race with a dogged no compromising determination.

It is Paul who describes metaphorically the life reality of a farmer, a soldier and, as we'll see here, of the athlete. In Eugene Peterson's THE MESSAGE translation, the book of Hebrews has a well-crafted set of words,

> "Do you see what this means—all these pioneers who blazed the way, all these veterans cheering us on? It means we'd better get on with it. Strip down, start running—and never quit! No extra spiritual fat, no parasitic sins. Keep your eyes on Jesus, who both began and finished this race we're in. **Study how he did it.** Because he never lost sight of where he was headed—that exhilarating finish in and with God— he could put up with anything along the way: cross, shame, whatever. And now he's there, in the place of honor, right alongside God." (Hebrews 12:1-2 THE MESSAGE)

That is a well-defined and wonderful model of pursuing God. Some years ago, Cheryl and I began an International School of the Psalmist, hosting meetings in various cities throughout the United States and many other countries of the world. We dug out many of the truths that are cataloged in these pages. We've always taught Biblical foundations coupled with practical, personal and team structured training. Countless churches where we've ministered have been gloriously changed because they've become worshipping churches. John Maxwell teaches, "Everything rises and falls on leadership."[2] An orchestra needs a conductor. When leadership moves toward God through intimate worship, everything changes.

Now, having invested teaching into a couple of dozen countries and having spent many years as a Founding Senior Pastor in Daytona Beach, Florida, I find that this pursuit of song and excellence lies still unsatisfied. The age old challenge remains at large in the church. Where are the anointed psalmists, singers and minstrels who we read of in Psalms, Chronicles and throughout the insights of the book of Revelation? Why are some churches addicted to so much entertainment now? Where's

---

[2]2007, John Maxwell, *The 21 Indispensable Qualities of a Leader*, Thomas Nelson, Inc.

their hunger? Certainly Heaven is not looking or waiting for the top ten self-promoted, hyped stars of the day to give God some attention. God's attention is reserved for those who have learned to worship in spirit and truth as Jesus said in John's Gospel.[3] The throne room shares no glory.

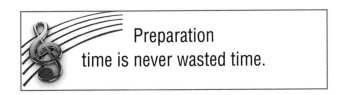

Preparation time is never wasted time.

I believe that this investment into your quest of the lifestyle of excellence will net great results of personal growth. You will be a blessing in your local church or ministry involvement. Your gift and heart effort will have such wonderful eternal value as you develop. King David demanded a high cost factor in his own pursuit for God's presence.[4] We know worship will NEVER cease. Your present preparation is necessary. Preparation time is never wasted time. One day, not too long from now, all believers will be worshipping together and enjoying a firsthand close-up look at our King.

These thoughts and methods once implemented are not a destination, but a lifestyle. Go for God's best in all you do. Lives are at stake and your intense worship of God is such a wonderful witness.

Note that each chapter title generally has an italicized verb in the heading. Verbs are action words. Italics are inserted purposely to help you know that, as you pursue the element, you also have a large part to play, no pun intended. Faith without works is DEAD.[5] Approach each chapter with a Biblical James—like attitude. These areas of pursuit are not simply cerebral. They demand action directed by your heart. I believe you'll enjoy every minute and fully accomplish all of God's desired results. I bless your reading and growth.

---

[3]Scripture Reference — John 4:24
[4]Scripture Reference — 2 Samuel 24:24
[5]Scripture Reference — James 2:17

CHAPTER TWO

OPEN DOOR

I ventured into music at an early age. Actually, I was born at an early age. I say ventured, but essentially there was little else for me to do. I had severe asthma as a young kid and didn't get to play outside a lot, at least, not like I wanted to. My parents, Dan and Clyde Ingram, (yes, Mom's given name is Clyde Christine) both worked hard to provide for my older brother Ben and me. Ben was the athlete, loved outdoors, and was always getting us into trouble. I was to become the musician. Because of the asthma and being indoors a lot, I often listened to LP vinyl records, which included early Ray Charles, Oscar Peterson, Errol Garner, Thelonious Monk, and a new, avant-garde sound from a pianist named Dave Brubeck. I didn't know their names at the time, or anything about them, but liked what I heard on the LPs. Without a piano or keyboard, I'd sit up in bed, close my eyes, and play air piano as if it was me performing. The music in my ears and pretending through my fingers was taking me on an adventure, a musical pursuit adventure. Later, when Gage Music delivered the new Wurlitzer Spinet piano, I'd try to imitate what I heard on real keys. Challenged as I was naturally, the chase was in me. I had already adventured and was determined to go again for the real. The door was cracked open.

No matter what the style or song, I enjoyed hearing and working on it to make it happen through my fingers. As you know, training is so necessary. People often say, "Practice makes perfect," but that is only partially correct. Practice actually makes permanent, good or bad. If you practice wrong, it's later hard to change. As you'll learn, your focus and its repeated efforts must be on the right goals.

At the young age of twelve, I was allowed to play with several older jazz musicians and was soon playing in local area VFW and Moose Clubs functions. They promised my mom that they would protect me from the potential of sipping anything illegal. After persistent, "Please, please, please Mom…" requests, she allowed me to play a few times. These guys knew all the old standards of Nat King Cole, Frank Sinatra, and Dean Martin. I brought my bag of songs from Bobby Darin, Chubby Checker, and the Everly Brothers. It was a wonderful growth period for my musicianship. The family agreement was that I would not skip Sunday morning church, because I often played for the choir at the downtown big church. As Mom would often say, "Bless my son. He puts the town drunks to bed Saturday nights and plays *Oh How I Love Jesus* to some of the same folk the next morning." Dad didn't agree that I should be playing in honkey tonks as he called them, but mom had persuaded him, because I was getting experience playing. Of course, I was also bringing $25.00 a night home on Friday and Saturday nights. That seemed to appease Dad who worked at the local Post Office. Then came the summer of 1963 when I went to Florida State University's summer music camp.

I was excited to go this prestigious college camp and be able to be on such a large campus with musicians only. It felt momentarily like Heaven. I knew I didn't want to go home. However, soon I was confronted with the true meaning of the word excellence. I don't mean I had never seen, spoken, or used the word. I got challenged with the evidence of tremendous musical superiority in students who were much younger. I abruptly realized just how behind I was in learning music, reading, theory, and technique. Here were students who could read music flawlessly and play classical pieces that I had only tried to imitate. They knew about music theory, composition, and were writing songs themselves. I was stunned and somewhat breathless. How did these kids get such musical chops, ability, and such discipline? It didn't take me long to get an intense pursuit of music, a lifetime adventure. Once I had heard a true pianist or sat in on a reading session for jazz band, or heard a trained choir, I was more so hooked. My appetite was voracious. Here was another whole world of resources that I hadn't experienced. That was many, many measures and codas ago.

I say all that to explain that the door was now opened for pursuit of musical excellence. Truthfully, the pursuit of music is only a part of the bigger song. It was later that I found the real goldmine of excellence in music ministry, the pursuit of His presence. The audience of One is your finest adventure ever in regard to anything to do with releasing your thoughts on the carrier of music.

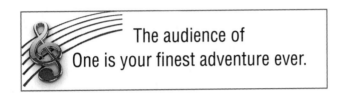

The audience of One is your finest adventure ever.

Ability, skill, and the understanding of complex musical compositions is the simple framework of a soul's heart toward God. In many conferences and seminars there's often discussion of ministry for God or to God. While both have awesome merits and value, your focus and true North compass should be to make your lifelong pursuit—His presence.

Using music as a tool for evangelism is brilliant. Likewise, having appropriate songs and sounds for altar times of salvation, dedication, or weddings, and funerals are all needed and acceptable. Being motivated in praise and stirred up with toe tapping infusion of gospel is always exhilarating. Certainly it would be unthinkable to sit at home around the fireplace during a season like Christmas in silence. We must hear *Joy to the World, Silent Night,* and *Oh Holy Night,* peppered with Vince Guaraldi's rendition of "Linus and Lucy" from *A Charlie Brown Christmas.*[6] The function of music is legitimate in all these cases. As long as we are positioned on this whole note in the galaxy, we'll be using music to serve us as entertainment or atmosphere.

---

[6] 1965 © Vince Guaraldi, "Linus and Lucy," "A Charlie Brown Christmas," *Hal Leonard Corporation*

The function of music brings notoriety for the carrier. Therein lies part of our dilemma. We're not here on earth just to become household names, but rather to bring our worship, (*weorthscipe,* old Anglo-Saxon term meaning "worth-ship,")[7] and honor to His Name. By default, we've all been guilty of attributing more importance to a name than the function or goal of our songs. I've already mentioned many famous writers and singers. No problem. We all have done that. It is A.W. Tozer's statement about worship that is the course correction for everyone, musician or not. He says that worship is, "...the missing jewel of the evangelical churches."[8] He states that the real treasure to pursue is the "Jewel of Worship." Many Christians are not even aware that the Father is seeking such who'll worship Him in Spirit and in Truth. They are "acluestic!"

I invite you to approach these next chapters as adjustments for an adventurous pursuit to establish foundational truths and skills that will stay with you throughout eternity. Just go ahead and open the door.

---

[7] 2011, en.wikepedia.org
[8] 1961, E. W. Tozer, "Worship the Missing Jewel of the Evangelical Church,"

CHAPTER THREE

DEVELOP FAITHFULNESS

The development process of faithfulness must be prefaced with a simple understanding. I know the challenge for musicians is not just learning their craft alone. Musicians often suffer with a wrong identity—their identification. I believe that once a person discovers who they really are IN Christ Jesus there is a wonderful transformation, and the perspective of our gifting changes. It is no longer for or about self. We discover that this lifestyle is about Him. The development of Bible faith coupled with the lifestyle of faithfulness is foremost regardless of what endeavor we're assigned. It is not our gift, our song, or our ability that will ever move mountains. Faithfulness and attention to Father God is essential. The truth of worship revealed in scripture becomes very apparent, "Thou art worthy, O Lord, to receive glory and honour and power: for thou hast created all things, and for thy pleasure they are and were created. (Revelation 4:11 KJV)

A NEW SEASON

From the end of the 20th Century and now into glory days of this new time frame, the world has seen several huge cultural shifts away from godliness. In the world, there has been a decline in Godly reverence and worship. Statistical researchers such as George Barna and others are declaring a major decline in traditional church-life worldwide.

Some say we are a post Christian nation in America. I believe, God laughs at such. Whether we all agree or not, we know that the Church at large HAS to reassess its awesome assignment and potential. We must as believing believers lay hold to a new season, howbeit short, as God's immense creative and loving expression through worship draws people into the knowledge of His Son. Anointed songs, regardless of style, draw people to something, or someone, hopefully Jesus Christ.

There is a Bible based plan for excellence that will never fail. The motive of pursuing God with your best cannot be overstated. The King deserves our best. Mediocrity has always been the enemy of best. I'm convinced that all believers are called to excellence in their giftings and ministries. God gave His best and we should do the same. Excellence is the basic form of Christianity.

EX*CEL*LENCE: WHAT IS IT?

Definition: noun[9]

1. The quality of being EXCELLENT
2. An excellent or valuable quality: VIRTUE

Many observations are available, and I have chosen a few to discuss.

- It is an attitude that God helps us develop.
- Excellence doesn't mean being perfect always.
- Excellence requires GREAT discipline.
- True excellence involves doing the best with the callings, gifts and opportunities that God gives us.

In the process of growing up in Christ Jesus, we must all find the place of daily conforming to His Word and finding the place of obedience in the Spirit. It is within your mind and heart that the battle for lordship is fought, or better said, surrendered. Jesus is Lord and always

---

[9]2011,www.thefreeDictionary.com/excellence

will be. As we mature in Him, we discover it is the details of this inner discipline that needs our undivided attention.

The quality of a product always depends on the quality of the materials used. God has placed His best in us so that we can mature and shine brightly. The Spirit of Grace awakens us to His intent and provision that resides in us, as we discover our gifts and their function.

The first thing we must establish is **faithfulness** in three areas. These are not exhaustive, but I believe are the most important; **His Word, vision and prayer.** Many would think it more necessary first to work on their craft—the song—voice technique or skills in playing scales, or perhaps spending more time listening to a favorite musical hero is a prerogative. I have found that helping musicians and singers establish this foundational truth first has more impact, because of the immediate, direct, effect on their heart for God. Whatever your heart is faithful to is what you will see develop. Your attention to daily faithfulness will attract more of the same. Maybe you have not been faithful in the Word, vision, or prayer, but I assure you, this is the surest way to grow with supernatural results. Understand that God has always committed His blessing to the faithful, not the talented or slick marketed ones. Likewise, it should be quite obvious that your enemy wants to keep the attention strictly on you and the exploitation of your gift for the flesh. The enemy wants your attention, and he promises great wages. The Bible calls his pay scale and early retirement program…death.

Paul told his protégé Timothy, "And the things that thou hast heard of me among many witnesses, the same commit thou to faithful men, who shall be able to teach others also." (2 Timothy 2:2 KJV) An excellent musician or singer has to settle this issue early. Developing faithfulness is God's plan.

HIS WORD

"The entrance of thy words giveth light; it giveth understanding unto the simple." (Psalm 119:130 KJV) Understand that ALL of the elements of music exist in the dimension of LIGHT. I marvel at the language of God. We are only now beginning to understand the essence of what happens in the light spectrum in regard to music. With the development of new scientific devices of measurement and advances in quantum physics, we now can understand more of the scriptural words "giveth light." There is more than just your auditory system hearing His Word coming into you. The sound itself gives you LIGHT! Yes, illumination is there but so much more. Psalmist/trumpeter/teacher, Phil Driscoll, has excelled in discovering and demonstrating this truth. The force of sound has a laser like ability to change molecules in sick bodies.

The spiritual adjustment here is to aid many musicians and singers to prioritize the entrance of His Word above their instrument or voice. So many church musicians and singers are aggressively faithful to their crafts while only slightly faithful to the Word of God. They spend hours rehearsing one phrase or scale and so little time hearing and acting on the Word. They will memorize a whole concert set of lyrics or progressions, but have yet to memorize and recall, "Jesus wept." (John 11:35 KJV) They know more about the owner's manual for their instruments than the Creator's manual for eternity. They can even recognize numerous songs by a few notes of an introduction, but have no recollection of their pastor's message from last Sunday. The mandate of the Spirit of Grace today is to spend more time in His Word and acting on it.

Your Bible speaks loudly, "This Book of the Law shall not depart out of your mouth, but you shall meditate on it day and night, that you may observe and do according to all that is written in it. For then you shall make your way prosperous, and then you shall deal wisely and have good success." (Joshua 1:8 AMP)

It's interesting to look into some of the methodology of King David's school of music. Students functioned on a 24-7 basis and were trained in all facets of spiritual and musical leadership. There is no substitute for hearing the Word, meditating on it and then acting on it through your voice or instrument. Of course, the Word of God is important in every believer's life regardless of calling. Become a student of the Word. Meditation in and on His Word should never be a casual thought. You are a priest with the awesome gift and tool of music. Your tool of music has a powerful stealth function that can transport the life changing Word of God to hurting people unaware. The more Word in you always brings life to your spirit and insights to your function as a psalmist. Mediating on His Word inside you makes your God bigger. That's a very good thing.

VISION

Become faithful in the area of **God's Vision**. Just as notes have place-
ment and timing in order to participate in the composition of a song,
God's plan for you has a similar function. You have to know what His
plan is. You must be faithful to God's vision for YOU! Vision's entrance,
volume, and pitch have to do with what God desires to be articulated.
Your value in the Kingdom plan is for you to sound off at the right place
and time. The Father is not just working on getting you a recording
deal or some popularity attention on a music hit chart. While there is
nothing wrong with the influence of recording labels and number one
hits, God's promotion is based on Kingdom principles. The purpose of
making a musician or singer well known or popular is to get His message known and to promote mankind's need of salvation. Hang up your
desire for fame and notoriety. This is a trap. God always commits to
faithfulness, not talent. Talent will only take you so far and, truthfully,
not very far in the real Kingdom of God. Artificial promotions are not
the key to success. His Vision is for you to be used to help bring, "…
deliverance to the captive." (Luke 4:18 KJV)

Wherever His vision has you going, that journey has real life. I
can attest to numerous times when my knowledge of God's vision for
our music ministry helped to minimize distractions and ridiculous, use-
less, rabbit trails. Not every invitation to go do something musically is
a God door opening. God's vision is based on the Kingdom mandate
to introduce His Love into this world. Your calling isn't given so you
can have a career or possess a fan club. This calling isn't so you'll have
a place to play or sing. Measure your understanding of the Kingdom
of God by these principles; (1) Does it show people the unconditional
Love of God? (2) Does it give them Godly hope or a path to an answer?
(3) Does it get them intimately involved with a growing relationship
with the Person of Jesus?

Another area is to become extremely attentive and faithful to your
Pastor's Vision. The fastest way of experiencing promotion in God is
to be faithful in another man's ministry. (Luke 16:12 KJV) Your pastor
has need of your gift functioning in line with his vision for the community where you live. Regardless of your present talent, your availability
to be trained and groomed is of utmost importance in the Kingdom.

Your pastor and leadership have been given the charge of training you so that you can do the work you are called to do. Many things in God are caught rather taught. Your observation may teach you more than you thought. Get in a pastor approved environment so you can grow.

You do have a pastor, right? You are in a local church, right? Sit, listen, study, be available, and volunteer even if it's in an area outside your gifting. It is there in serving that God can and will show Himself strong. Realize that a shepherd boy, David, had great potential and a wonderful gift. He stayed faithful to his dad by guarding sheep day and night while learning his craft on the hillside. Can you see him singing to dumb sheep who just loved every bad out of tune note? I say dumb lovingly, not derogatorily, because sheep are always to be led, never herded. Sheep follow. They can't be driven.

David was faithful there first, before a single song was penned and in its revered place in your Bible. He was certainly not known or famous during those hidden days on the mountainside. His worldwide ministry was only a hillside effort, but I believe it was the original HillSong! The local Jerusalem Temple A&R people were not looking for his songs. Surrounded by smelly sheep and their "baa-baa" monotone applause, David remained faithful.

Your present situation may be similar. It's only for a season. I remind you that David authored much of the largest book in your Bible and possesses the only reference in the Bible to being the, "...sweet psalmist of Israel." (2 Samuel 23:1 KJV) Stay daily faithful to your pastor's vision. Make him or her happy and put a smile on their face by being faithful.

The other focus of faithfulness is to **Your Vision.** I don't think most musicians and singers have a problem with this. In fact, it may have been a part of your conversation just today. It should be positioned last, following God's Vision, and Your Pastor's vision, so that it is in its right perspective. Obviously, it is important to God or He would have not placed the desire and gifting in you. Don't be too quick to call it quits when things don't happen in a few days, months or even years. Be faithful to pray about it and expect it to manifest. Take a break now and write out what God has spoken to you about your future. I recommend you write some specific details. You could write things like where you're going to live, or who you'll marry, or what size house you'll have. Concentrate, rather, on a concise headline of what God wants from His ministry through you. Those others pieces of the puzzle will come in due time. As you write, make it in Technicolor®, describing exactly what you see He has for you! Habakkuk shares that we should take care of the business of our future by looking to God. Here's his story: (Bold is for emphasis.)

> "I will stand upon my watch, and set me upon the tower, and will watch to see what he will say unto me, and what I shall answer when I am reproved. And the LORD answered me, and said, write the **vision**, and make *it* plain upon tables, that he may run that readeth it. For the **vision** *is* yet for an appointed time, but at the end it shall speak, and not lie: though it tarry, wait for it; because it will surely come, it will not tarry. Behold, his soul *which* is lifted up is not upright in him: but the just shall live by his faith." (Habakkuk 2:1-4 KJV)

The MESSAGE TRANSLATION states it with yet more insight and clarity:

> "What's God going to say to my questions? I'm braced for the worst. I'll climb to the lookout tower and scan the horizon. I'll wait to see what God says, how he'll answer my complaint. And then GOD answered: "Write this. Write what you see. Write it out in big block letters so that it can be read on the run. This **vision**—message is a witness pointing to what's coming. It aches for the coming—it can hardly wait! And it doesn't lie. If it seems slow in coming, wait. It's on its way. It will come right on time. Look at that man, bloated by self-importance—full of himself but soul-empty. But the person in right standing before God through loyal and steady believing is fully alive, really alive."

Note the resolve found in verse two, "Write in big block letters." Verse three states, "It can hardly wait and it won't lie!" That ought to stir you up as to your potential. Stop and shout! Thank God. My vision is manifesting.

MY VISION

Years ago as we began this ministry, I wrote these words as to what I felt Cheryl and I would be doing till we got to Heaven. One day we may be a part of the teaching team up there too. The statement is simple, and we've stayed faithful to it, although God added to our assignment the role of pastors some years ago. It reads in part that we will be, "… teaching musical and spiritual excellence to today's psalmists." That was thirty plus years ago. We developed dogged faithfulness, wouldn't quit, and now I am able to visit your mind and heart through these words. Faithfulness is a necessity. No compromise, no laziness and certainly no quit. Norvel Hayes often says, "God don't never bless lazy Christians."

When I was first invited to join the Kenneth Copeland Crusade Team, I remember Brother Copeland would tell the now famous story from Oral Roberts, his mentor and father in the faith. The account, as I remember, was that Kenneth, who was around age thirty at the time, was one of the airplane pilots for Oral Robert's Crusade Team. His responsibilities included accompanying him to each meeting, driving him from the plane to the hotel and then to the meetings and back. He had been instructed not to engage Brother Roberts in any conversation and to speak only when spoken to. On one occasion as they were driving to a meeting, suddenly Brother Roberts blurted out in the car, "Kenneth, do you know how to be a success in God?" Stunned and not knowing exactly how to answer or if he even should, Brother Copeland momentarily hesitated. Oral Roberts continued in that strong anointed voice, "Find out the will of God for your life, confer no longer with flesh and blood and then get the job done at any cost."

Now many years later, that truth spoken in a car with just those two men is able to be shared again with the same power. As you read this, refresh your mind; (1) WHAT HAS GOD TOLD YOU TO DO? (2) DON'T LET FAMILY OR ANYONE TALK YOU OUT OF IT. (3) GET IT DONE NO MATTER WHAT IT COSTS YOU! Stay faithful to that vision part that is YOU! So what if it takes years? So what if there's opposition? Abraham was very old before getting much done for God. Moses had been a basket case at one time. Joseph had major family problems and still went from the pit to the palace. Lazarus was just glad that he had a friend in Jesus. God had a plan for them and God has a plan for you. You can do this.

PRAYER

It is unrealistic to assume that there will be any ministry of substance without developing the discipline of prayer. Worship celebrates the presence of God in intimacy and likewise prayer is another facet of intimacy. Unlike a song structure of a determined set of musical bars, prayer can be a continuous flow of closeness. It is as E. M. Bounds said, "No learning can make up for the failure to pray. No earnestness, no diligence, no study, no gifts will supply its lack."[10] It is an integral part of the priestly role of musicians and singers. You can gain great strength and wonderful insights to the complexities and nuances of God while in prayer.

Every public corporate service needs musicians and singers interceding for it on a regular basis. It should never be the last thing we do. Pray in agreement for God to move in every song to every member. Pray that every song blesses and stirs the heart of your pastor. Pray for supernatural recall of lyrics, notes and chords so that your thinking of notes doesn't impede your worshipping. I have found musical notes—answers—many late nights as a pianist/arranger, because I am willing and disciplined to pray about everything. Insights to arrangements, voicings, chords and even complex technical audio problems suddenly become clear when I mediate and allow the Holy Spirit to pray the answer through me. Moreover, it is so refreshing to enjoy the Father's lap time without a single note or lyric. Become a faithful minister of prayer.

The One who called you into ministry has never been unfaithful. Your faith pleases God and puts a big smile on His face. It's a joy to see psalmists develop in this arena. Being faithful and loyal are excellent qualities to be known for. You are punctual and on time for all rehearsals and other facets of ministry. A minister once told me that being twenty minutes late equates to a twenty minute lie. If you give your word to be somewhere at a certain time—be there. My motto is

---

[10]2011, E. M. Bounds, "Power Through Prayer," www.prayerfoundation.org

the only way to be on time is to be early. Be there early prepared to start on the downbeat. Can you imagine your lack of trust for a fellow musician who is always late, not just to show up, but with their notes or rhythm as well? Maybe the drummer has a timing issue with a certain style and always blows it or has a train wreck with a certain song. It would annoy you until it got fixed. Every sluggish musical spirit impedes excellence until dealt with and corrected. In Chapter 5, *Develop* Skillfulness, you'll find a plan for growing in musical abilities, thus eliminating the frustration that mediocrity brings.

In the early days of our School of the Psalmist, I started using a scripture based confession that has helped thousands of students, young and old, establish identity as to who they are. Although it is printed here, stop. Take a short break. Go get your Bible and underline or highlight this passage for yourself. Stop…have you got your Bible? Paul loved his son in the Lord, Timothy. I know because he was always encouraging and mentoring him with a lot of grace. That's a good thing. I trust you'll be like Timothy and take this to heart. There is a powerful description of the Body of Christ nestled in Paul's second letter to Timothy. Look at Paul's words to Timothy,

> "But in a great house there are not only vessels of gold and of silver, but also of wood and of earth; and some to honour, and some to dishonour. If a man therefore purge himself from these, he shall be a vessel unto honour, sanctified, and meet for the master's use, *and* prepared unto every good work. Flee also youthful lusts: but follow righteousness, faith, charity, peace, with them that call on the Lord out of a pure heart." (2 Timothy 2: 20-22 KJV) Eugene Peterson's THE MESSAGE really illuminates this:
>
> "In a well-furnished kitchen there are not only crystal goblets and silver platters, but waste cans and compost buckets—some containers used to serve fine meals, others to take out the garbage. Become the kind of container God can use to present any and every kind of gift to his guests for their blessing. Run away from infantile indulgence. Run after mature righteousness—faith, love, peace—joining

those who are in honest and serious prayer before God." What I want you to have is a clear focus on WHO YOU ARE as a musician—singer—psalmist. The following confession is a very useful, daily, tool that keeps your attention on being faithful, living clean and being prepared spiritually and musically. Insert your name here:

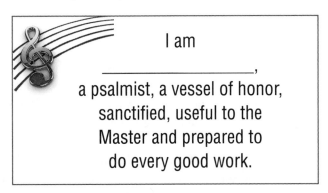

> I am
>
> _____,
>
> a psalmist, a vessel of honor,
> sanctified, useful to the
> Master and prepared to
> do every good work.

I am a vessel of Honour—honorable people are on time, faithful and trustworthy. They keep their word and have a great character. *Sanctified*—You are set apart spiritually and live holy into God. *Meet for the Master's use*—The Amplified Bible states that verse as, "… useful for honorable and noble purposes." The Father God deems you useful. *Prepared unto every good work*—You have practiced, studied and prepared yourself so that when needed by God, you're ready to do a good work!

Take the time to rewrite this and place it on a prominent place—your dressing mirror, refrigerator or at your desk so it can be daily read. This reminder needs to be viewed many times during the day. Make yourself a post card or a computer screen saver of it and tell others who YOU ARE! Faithfulness covers a very broad area of life. Become legendary as a faithful person. It is an awesome quality, and is a foundational part of excellence.

Faithfulness is inherent to your pursuit of God. There should not be any compromise in your efforts here. To further aid your study in regard to faithfulness, review, meditate, and mark these scriptures in your own Bible for their importance:

- "_____ to shew thyself approved unto God, a _____ that needeth not to be ashamed, rightly dividing the word of truth." (2 Timothy 2:15 KJV)
- "But without _____ it is impossible to _____ Him. For he that cometh to God must believe He is, and that He is a rewarder of them that diligently seek him." (Hebrews 11:6 KJV)
- "But ye, beloved, building up _____ on your most Holy _____." (Jude 20 KJV)
- "For this cause have I sent unto you Timotheus, who is my beloved son, and _____in the Lord, who shall bring you into remembrance of my ways which be in Christ, as I _____ every where in every church." (1 Corinthians 4:17 KJV)
- "And I thank Christ Jesus our Lord, who hath enabled me, for that he counted me _____, putting me into the ministry..." (1 Timothy 1:12 KJV)
- Now make this confession:

"Today, I make a determination to be found FAITHFUL in what God has called me to do. I do so with resolve. I am being fully developed in FAITHFULNESS."

CHAPTER FOUR

PRACTICE HOLINESS

We're living in a time when it seems that charisma is much more applauded than character. It is sad that people in the public arena, entertainers, politicians, sports celebrities and others have reputations which are empty shells lacking any spiritual moral compass. Likewise, some churches promote the use of questionable characters who have talent, instead of seasoned honorable believers who are living Godly. In some cases, church leadership seems to have scales on their eyes and ears. They pay worldly people to do Kingdom business. They've been fooled into thinking that as long as someone can move a crowd, its ok. Well, I firmly believe God still has and always has had a high standard of holiness. You must practice holiness, working to keep your life pleasing unto God.

I remember when I first heard Dr. Ed Cole, a prominent minister to men well before any of the current men's groups existed. Cheryl and I were doing the music for his national conference in Washington, DC. He spoke so powerfully often punctuating his message with colloquialisms, which were short sermons in a single sentence. He made the statement, "Reputation is what men think of you, but your character is what God knows of you."[11] Your Bible says, "...without Holiness,

---

[11]2011, "Coleisms—the Ed Cole ® Library," www.edcole.org

no man shall see God..." (Hebrews 12:14 KJV) We must see music ministry once again become CLEAN, character driven and not reputation driven. In truth, why would any leader tolerate the dangerous, explosive, potential of the effect of ungodliness and its fruit? What is to be gained by ungodly living? I submit absolutely nothing, but there is contrastingly much to lose.

To aid you in this pursuit of holiness, let's focus on some basic elements of your music ministry for a moment. The reason you're studying and growing today is because God has called you and you have answered by saying yes. He believes in you. Your pastor believes in you, and so do I. None of His plans for you have defeat in them.

The only element that can bring about defeat or uselessness is YOUR participation in doubt, unbelief and/or willful disobedience. It is extremely disappointing when any believer falls from grace or has some kind of moral, financial, or emotional failure. It was disappointing when David failed, but he quickly repented. Generally, these circumstances come about because of a lack of spiritual oversight, a lack of character or an undisciplined mind. I've heard it said for years in a derogatory attitude toward musicians and singers, "Well you know how they are. They're temperamental!" To which I reply, "Yes, half temper and half mental." We must change that erroneous perception.

Another one of Dr. Ed Cole's "Coleisms,"[12] though a rather broad statement, clarifies my point. "Life is composed by our CHOICES and constructed by our WORDS." As we engage each day, our conscience choices must all be filtered by the Word and the Holy Spirit. The Word and the Holy Spirit help us construct the framework for speaking life producing words. Living a life of holiness is a daily choice. In truth, the choice is already made when you settle it in your heart to always honor your covenant in Christ Jesus.

Ministry, regardless of call or function, in itself demands a high value on holiness. Paul explained it to Timothy, his young student in training, with strong language, " [*For it is He*] Who delivered and saved us and called us with a calling in itself holy and leading to

---

[12]ibid

holiness [*to a life of consecration, a vocation of holiness*]; [*He did it*] not because of anything of merit that we have done, but because of and to further His own purpose and grace (unmerited favor) which was given us in Christ Jesus before the world began [*eternal ages ago*]." (2 Timothy 1:9 AMP)

Did you catch that? He has called us with a calling, "...in itself holy and leading to holiness [*to a life of consecration, a vocation of holiness*]." Even the Prophet Isaiah underscores when speaking of the Kingdom of God, "And a highway shall be there, and a way; and it shall be called the Holy Way. The unclean shall not pass over it, but it shall be for the redeemed; the wayfaring men, yes, the simple ones and fools, shall not err in it and lose their way." (Isaiah 35:8a KJV) We're on a highway called Holy, the road of priesthood.

Society has generally tried to lower the bar of righteousness and civility particularly in musicians and singers. In the world, we've been called on to entertain and exploit whatever the flesh desires, thus creating a self-gratifying lifestyle. However, in the Kingdom of God, the motivation is to magnify the King and His Kingdom, and it demands that we be like the King. Thank God! I've observed through years of garage bands, concerts, studio sessions, and every other kind of venue the ruin of a gifted person, simply because their source of inspiration and creativity was wrong. Smoking, drinking, and in general wrong stimulants destroy the physical body as well as pollute the mind and distort rational thinking. When you solidify Father God and the Kingdom as your source of inspiration, the greed and need of your flesh dissipates. It is strangely wonderful. You have the Creator working on your inside. You find that you don't lose your ability to play various styles of music by abstaining from chemical stimuli. In fact, you gain a different motivation. I'll discuss this

Living clean and having a healthy reputation of influence is so vital to a ministry of excellence.

more in detail in Chapter 6 *Desire* and *Cultivate* Creativeness.

Living clean and having a healthy reputation of influence is so vital to a ministry of excellence. All the talent, finely crafted abilities, wonderful lyrics and writing skills become magnified a thousand-fold because of the power of holiness. Holiness brings more anointing, because of the vessel's usefulness to the Father.

As we'll later discover in other chapters, the ministry of music and its heavenly guidelines were first instituted during King David's reign. His, and many other insights with respect to plans, purposes and pursuits are given as wonderful examples. One written in the Book of Nehemiah particularly comes to mind and gives valuable thoughts about holiness. I have taught this passage for many years, underscoring how the priests of the Lord first **separated** themselves, and then took an **oath** to God. They were compensated receiving grain, fruit, and tithe offerings and later **vowed** to never forsake the House of God.

> "And the rest of the people, the priests, the Levites, the porters, the singers, the Nethinims, and all they that had **separated themselves** from the people of the lands unto the law of God, their wives, their sons, and their daughters, every one having knowledge, and having understanding; They clave to their brethren, their nobles, and entered into a curse, and into an **oath**, to walk in God's law, which was given by Moses the servant of God, and to observe and do all the commandments of the LORD our Lord, and his judgments and his statutes; (Nehemiah 10:28-30 KJV) For the children of Israel and the children of Levi shall bring the offering of the corn, of the new wine, and the oil, unto the chambers, where *are* the vessels of the sanctuary, and the priests that minister, and the porters, and the singers: and **we will not forsake the house of our God**." (Nehemiah 10:39 KJV)

What a great example of the priesthood and its determination to be sanctified and set apart. In Nehemiah 10:29, the word oath is *sheb-oo-aw'* or *sheba*—seven, the perfect number.[13] These musicians and singers promised, under oath, to never forsake the House of God. I think that maybe we should revisit that thought. While you don't need to make a doctrinal position out of it, I believe there should be agreement made to put the House of God first place, never forsaking it.

Now as to the obvious dichotomy of kinds of music ministry, I understand that many are called to various outreaches within the evangelistic field. Musical evangelism is a valid form of ministry. However, musicians are not called to mirror the world, but to influence it. We are, as Jesus stated, the salt and light. Every music minister, regardless of platform style, needs to be planted in a home church and be submitted and committed to a pastor. You should support your home church and participate in services, as schedules allow. Your responsibility is to tithe there and pray for it. It is a holy place where you can hear from God and be trained and prepared for excellence in music ministry.

I remember some years ago, Cheryl and I were participating in a twenty-seven hour nation changing praise and worship event in Gothenburg, Sweden. There were three sound crews each working eight hour shifts. The band Jerusalem, Phil Driscoll, the world famous guitarist, Mike Deasy, a national Swedish artist, Carola Maria Häggkvist, and a whole host of church musicians and teams from across Sweden were given license to lead the people in intercessory prayer and praise—all directed at seeing their country turn to God. The arena held approximately eight thousand.

The day after this momentous gathering of musicians and prayer intercessors, Cheryl and I met a pastor for lunch. We walked around an indoor city mall and heard a familiar sound of guitar music at the end of the hall. It was anointed and there was quite a crowd. Upon investigation, we discovered Mike Deasy, playing as if a typical street musician, although he was witnessing and praying for people and doing the work of an evangelist. Musical evangelism doesn't always require a big stage.

No believer should feel isolated from the world, but certainly with a lifestyle of holiness, we are insulated from its affect. Although

---

[13]James Strong, "The Exhaustive Concordance of The Bible", Hebrew #7621

many preach separation from the world in a religious regulatory way, we should never be isolated from people. If it's your calling to go into the world marketplace then do it with strong principle. You are on a fishing trip, a mission, using your gift as a drawing tool or magnet. You should never allow the world to put you back in the water to become food for the sharks.

I've heard Dr. Mark T. Barclay, former Marine Corps Sergeant and Senior Founding Pastor of Living Word Church in Midland, Michigan, say a simple truth that fits for this chapter, "This Bible is not just readable. It's really livable!" How powerful. Commit yourself afresh and anew to be a person of honor, integrity, and above all, live holy before God, your family, and your peers. Here are few closing thoughts for consideration.

- Holiness is not freedom from temptation, but it is the power to overcome.
- Holiness is a virtue that often vanishes when you talk about it, but becomes gloriously conspicuous when you silently live it.
- "Follow peace with all men, and holiness, without which no man shall see the Lord." (Hebrews 12:14 KJV)
- Only YOU can damage your character.
- Reputation is precious, but character is priceless.
- A flaw in one's character will show up under pressure.

CHAPTER FIVE

MAINTAIN SENSITIVITY TO THE HOLY SPIRIT

Sensitivity to the Third Person of the Trinity is one of the most important elements for excellence in music ministry. In fact, it's essential for all believing believers. The Holy Spirit is the Teacher of the Church. We must hear, obey and be particularly sensitive to all His instructions. It is a good thing, especially for musicians and singers. We understand the function and role of conductors, as we are generally taught to be followers. The Holy Spirit is the Conductor. Pay attention.

In the very beginning when God created sound and light with the words, "Let there be LIGHT…," (Genesis 1:1 KJV) the Holy Spirit of God was involved. He knows sound and has always been involved in producing this wonderful tool of communication between spirit beings. In every ministry effort, His presence and insights are needed. You, as a vessel of honor, need to be able to flow with your pastor as a part of the platform ministry. The Holy Spirit stands available to aid you. Whether in church worship, personal concert selections, or street music ministry you need to hear instructions from the Holy Spirit. In learning to sing or play, you can have the most qualified resident Teacher on your insides. Every area of a ministry of excellence needs this valuable Third Person of the Godhead.

With that short overview statement, let's look at the Gospel of John which reads, "But the Comforter (Counselor, Helper, Intercessor,

Advocate, Strengthener, Standby), the Holy Spirit, Whom the Father will send in My name [*in My place, to represent Me and act on My behalf*], He will teach you all things. And He will cause you to recall (will remind you of, bring to your remembrance) everything I have told you." (John 14:26 AMP)

Any singer or musician who is pursuing a ministry of excellence must pay close attention here. As gifted artists fully understand, we love to create and then perform. It's part of our framework. The Holy Spirit is always looking for people who desire to flow with the plan of the Father. A song list or program, even birthed in prayer, is subject to change by the Conductor. John says, "A time will come, however, indeed it is already here, when the true (genuine) worshipers will worship the Father in spirit and in truth (reality); for the Father is seeking just such people as these as His worshipers. God is a Spirit (a spiritual Being) and those who worship Him must worship Him in spirit and in truth (reality)." (John 4:23-24 AMP)

These are Jesus words and cannot be discounted or watered down. If you have a red letter edition, they appear in red because Christ spoke them. I love the fact that Father God is seeking us. We need to use our spiritual GPS tracking system to locate that place where we're worshipping in spirit and truth. I'm certain things will change for us in that place. I'm also reminded that God is, "...a rewarder of those who diligently seek Him..." (Hebrews 11:6 KJV) and now He's seeking us. Phew! What a place to be led of the Spirit of God.

- Wilt thou not revive us again: that thy people may rejoice in thee? (Psalm 85:6 KJV)
- Shew us thy mercy, O LORD, and grant us thy salvation. (Psalm 85:7 KJV)
- I will hear what God the LORD will speak: for he will speak peace unto his people, and to his saints: but let them not turn again to folly. (Psalm 85:8 KJV)
- Surely his salvation *is* nigh them that fear him; that glory may dwell in our land. (Psalm 85:9 KJV)
- Mercy and truth are met together; righteousness and peace have kissed each other. (Psalm 85:10 KJV)

The Sons of Korah wrote a wonderful picturesque song for the Chief Musician in the Temple. Look again at verse ten of Psalm 85. Mercy and truth are now together. Righteousness and peace have been positioned to kiss. What a magnificent scene of flowing in the Spirit of Grace. We should all desire to be in that kind of flow. There is no greater intimate moment than when God's righteousness and carefree peace embrace in a kiss.

I have had numerous experiences when the Teacher would aid me in writing songs, helping me to work out complex chord progressions. The Helper has greatly assisted me in understanding the digital technological forest of midi, sound files, and digital audio mixes. Early in my music ministry as a studio arranger, I experienced these real God moments of writing arrangements for recordings. Thank God, that since then, I've had many more as well. Listening back to some of my older music arrangements, I am so blessed to say with true humility the Spirit of God knew what was needed, and I listened and obeyed Him.

In 1980, as pianist/arranger with Kenneth Copeland Ministries, I had the pleasure of working with a brilliant producer, Darrell Glenn. We had collaborated on many songs and music projects in Florida at Central Sound Studios. One day he showed me a song originally entitled, *I am Jehovah*, which later was correctly re-titled, *He is Jehovah*. It was written at the kitchen table of the wonderful country psalmist and minister, Betty Jean Robinson. During one series of studio sessions, I was preparing this particular song for an upcoming recording project for Kenneth Copeland. The groove of the song had to be energetic, classy and orchestrated. The original demo, which I still have on cassette and archived, had been done in a somewhat country, two beat, predictable and simplistic style.

That evening and for several days and nights afterwards, I would write with the intent of making this a distinctive and noteworthy arrangement. I pressed God for ideas and the Holy Spirit joyfully obliged. For example, in order to keep a hint of the original blue grass style, I used a simple mandolin opening for a few bars and then suddenly a huge orchestral sustained chord before the first verse. It worked well as Brother Copeland's classic voice came in over a wood block click type rhythmic sound for the first verse. Later in the song and rather unexpectedly for a typical song length, I had the song arrangement stop as if it was over. Then the rhythm joyfully restarted with timbales and percussion, which was played on the recording by Alex Acuna. A funky groove bass line, was played by Abraham Laboriel, and Bill Maxwell set the groove with the drums. These members of the band Koinonia are well respected Christian studio musicians and it was an honor to work with them. In recording the lead vocal, just before the verse vocally restarted, Brother Copeland gave a deep, "Huh—huh," as a chuckle signifying absolute assurance of who the Father is, *He is Jehovah.* Just as he completed that, a two note trill half step string phrase helped to build suspense along with two contrasting lines of French horns and trumpets ascending and descending simultaneously. It would later become a classic arrangement. The format and performance really worked as Kenneth Copeland ministered it in conventions, churches, television and radio. The song has been played in thousands of churches and has sold multiplied thousands worldwide. Vocalist, Kenneth Copeland, Producer, Darrell Glenn, and I were blessed that it was nominated for a Grammy Award later that year.

You must grab this truth that the Creator has great insights and information via the Holy Spirit. Of all the creative people on the face of the earth, you should desire, welcome, and fellowship with the Holy Spirit daily. Look at another example of the value of sensitivity and obedience of the Holy Spirit.

You, as a minister of the Gospel in song, are a part of a ministerial team. It is the goal of every true pastor, or hopefully should be, that God show up in the service. You're not at church just to sing three fast songs, one medium song, and then three slow songs, have a few annoying announcements, followed by a three point sermon and a poem. When the flock assembles, the Good Shepherd desires to impart revelation, good news, and deliverance to His sheep. God desires to inhabit the praises of His people. He does it through excellent ministers like you, vessels of honor, who are prepared to do every good work.

Under leadership of a chief musician, a music director, the worship team should always be maturing in their ability to minister with excellence and enjoy the songs of the Lord. Given the trust and permission released by the senior pastor, the team can develop spiritually and musically with regard to the pastor's vision for that church body.

Sing songs that stir his/her heart and are in line with his/her flow, not just some typical current top ten song list. It is extremely important to practice chord changes, work on vocal blend, and learn to flow together as a team. In those times of preparation, it's also wonderful and highly recommended to spend time learning to sing and flow in the Spirit. The ability to take a thought, or respond spontaneously with accurate spiritual and musical excellence doesn't just happen. This is why you need to learn to be sensitive to the Holy Spirit.

If you've communed and learned to respond to a nudge of the Holy Spirit during private preparation times, then later in a corporate worship time the song of the Lord can be brought forth. That is always a refreshing moment. It can also bless a whole congregation of folk who probably will think that it was well planned and rehearsed. Regardless, it can bless all.

Here's a personal example. I've known many times before a service started that our prepared song list was just a starting point. We had a musical plan, but I would sense in my spirit that we might not really finish this song list. Then as the service progressed, there would be a stirring and a musical phrase would come to mind. Since I function predominately as a psalmist/pastor using my keyboards as my main tool, my spiritual mind would begin to discern a score or musical progression and instinctively my hands would respond. Let me hasten to say, this isn't some special anointed gift for me alone. I have opened my heart to a higher Conductor of song and trained my brain to hush and go with the moment. There's plenty of scripture to suggest for us all to sing a new song. I am providing a partial list of reference resources at the back of this book. I do believe with all my heart that everyone who desires God can learn to flow in this regard.

My wife, Cheryl, has developed this flow of the spirit in a masterful way. Often in her psalmist ministry she releases a song melody and lyrics on the given progression that I am playing. She says she is listening intently to what I am playing. That's the wonderful part. I am listening to what she is singing. The two marry, if you will, and once the song takes form, it is then easy for the singers, band and congregation to pick up on it. The song of the Lord birthed from heaven always refreshes and causes joy. It's as if a fresh wind of God's presence sweeps through.

I pause here to offer a note of prudence in regard to submission to authority in the service regarding spontaneous song. It should not be construed as control as to why a pastor establishes guidelines. Flow with your leadership, and do not assume that you should interrupt that service, just because you have a prompting of the Spirit. Every service should have a purpose and order. Pastors are given Holy Spirit led direction for the congregation. Be sensitive to the pastor's authority. The timing of when and where it happens in the service should also be considered. Attention and obedience to leadership is extremely important, regardless of what you may sense. Just because you have a nudging or feeling, doesn't mean that in these moments you shouldn't still submit to the appropriate leadership. Sometimes a prophetic song you receive is actually for another moment and you need to be aware so you don't cause confusion. I've had songs come during a service, and later at the close, been able to share them when it would make more sense. Learn to gently flow with the Father and your leadership.

The whole concept of flowing in the song of the Lord may sound strange for some whose theological structure doesn't permit such. That is understandable. Maybe you sense a Holy Spirit sensitivity of flow simply in the selection of songs, which is very important as well. Hear from Heaven for your situation.

In truth whether rehearsed or spontaneous, there should be a discernable flow of the Holy Spirit in every arena of worship, from the various structured liturgical circles, to blended services, to a full-gospel shout the walls down service, to a simple southern evangelical meeting. Regardless of the venue or style, an anointed music ministry of excellence is designed to undergird the move of God's Spirit. If there is no distinguishable appearance of God's Spirit, then why are we doing this?

Excellence in music ministry demands positive communication between leadership and psalmists. If you or your team has not had these discussions with your leadership, ask for a meeting and get their direction. Your desire to flow with the Spirit and grow personally in the song of the Lord should speak volumes. Work together as a team—pastor and musicians/singers. Get to know your members spiritually. Rehearsals should be more than musical. Have some teaching moments, as well as group prayer. The very essence of all corporate worship and the use of music as a part of its system must be Holy Spirit led. As I heard psalmist/teacher/pastor, Ray Hughes, once say, "Learn to flow in the Holy Ghost, not just jerk."

I suggest that you do some homework yourself as to learning and growing in your understanding of what real worship service and ministry is. Unfortunately in these last sixty plus years, our society has declined globally in its understanding of God and consequently of recognizing true worship. Jesus gave his short workshop session on worship seen in your Bible in the fourth chapter of the book of John. Here we read the story of Jesus stopping for some well water and sending the disciples in for some fish and chips. He has an encounter with a local woman with a loose reputation who is gathering water. Jesus turns the conversation to worship. Like so many people, she tries to be a bit religious, so as to hide her own lack of knowledge and sin condition.

> "But the hour cometh, and now is, when the true worshippers shall worship the Father in **spirit and in truth**: for the **Father seeketh such** to worship him. God is a Spirit: and they that worship him must worship *him* in spirit and in truth." (John 4:23-24 KJV)

It is imperative that we return to real worship, not a better program or song list. When something is void of God, it's dead. In some circles, it appears that the horse of praise and worship is dead. Why is it that movements become monuments? Why do we relegate our formulas to what we have already experienced? Worship with no anointing has little reason to exist except that it supports tradition. The Holy Conductor is very creative. It really doesn't matter whether you get a better saddle, a new blanket under the saddle, or change the reins. If the horse is dead, then get another horse. Don't invest in saddles.

Maybe this is too drastic of an idea for some, but true excellence requires **worshipping in spirit and in truth.** You know this. God is a Spirit, and we must never let song lists, performance or ritual try to do what the Holy Spirit is more than capable of doing through us. Consider these few famous credible quotes from a strong advocate of worship,

A.W. Tozer, who speaks with a heart of compassion for the Church to regain its pursuit of God and His worship:

- "If Bible Christianity is to survive the present world upheaval, we shall need to recapture the spirit of worship."
- "The Church has surrendered her once lofty concept of God and has substituted for it one so low, so ignoble, as to be utterly unworthy of thinking, worshipping men."
- "I wonder if there was ever a time when true spiritual worship was at a lower ebb. To great sections of the Church the art of worship has been lost entirely, and in its place has come that strange and foreign thing called the 'program.' This word has been borrowed from the stage and applied with sad wisdom to the type of public service which now passes for worship among us."
- "We have lost our spirit of worship and our ability to withdraw inwardly to meet God in adoring silence."[14]

Years ago while living in Ft Worth, Texas, I attended a music conference in which I heard Judson Cornwall, an awesome vessel of honor and the Word. He makes this statement that helps clarify the need for Holy Spirit sensitivity, "Whenever the method of worship becomes more important than the Person of worship, we have already prostituted our worship. There are entire congregations who worship praise and praise worship but who have not yet learned to praise and worship God in Jesus Christ."[15]

I'm challenged as I write to think how many times I may have missed the divinely inspired flow of Heaven all because my favorite song was on the list. I love that song. Everyone worshiped and the congregation was in step with us, but I wonder, did God receive it? I've learned that God will allow you to have your own little service. Perhaps He may be more comfortable, though, inhabiting the praises at a different gathering where people aren't concerned about the songs they like, but

---

[14] 1952, A.W. Tozer, "The Art of True Worship," *Moody Monthly,* April Edition
[15] 1987, Judson Cornwall, "Worship As Jesus Taught It," *Victory House Publishers,* #70

only in loving HIM. He will be worshipped in spirit and in truth. We must stay sensitive to Him at all costs.

Remember Heaven once had a chief worship leader, and he chose wrongly not to flow with the Father. He disobeyed Heaven's protocol. He decided to make it about him, desiring the worship for himself. He was severely dismissed and banished in just a nanosecond. The Word says, "I beheld satan as lightning fall from heaven." (Luke 10:18 KJV) There were no discussions, no meetings and certainly no negotiations. He was gone!

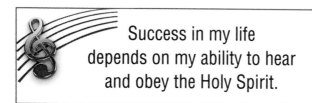

Success in my life depends on my ability to hear and obey the Holy Spirit.

Sensitivity to the Person of the Holy Spirit is vital for a ministry of excellence. Let's end this segment with a confession. I believe it will aid your spirit man to memorize and say this daily.

Success in my life depends on my ability to hear and obey the Holy Spirit.

CHAPTER SIX

DESIRE AND *CULTIVATE* CREATIVENESS

When one thinks of creativity, many historical giants like Michelangelo, Einstein, Mozart, or even King David and the great volumes of Psalms may come to mind. George F. Handel, the composer of *The Messiah*, hymnists like John Wesley, Ira Sankey, and Fanny Crosby, are also some iconic artists, and there are thousands more. Maybe you've enjoyed prolific gospel music writers such as Andraé Crouch, Bill and Gloria Gaither, and Israel Houghton. You can name your top ten. The real take home truth is that all sorts of people, including you, possess assorted levels of intelligence and natural ability, and are capable of engaging in a satisfying creative process. Just because you'll never be King David, Handel, or Andraé doesn't mean that you can't harness your God inspired ideas and create songs that will reach the world. Actually, God wants you to be you. He doesn't need another King David, Handel, or Andraé. God has things prepared to flow through you that no one else can receive. Believe it! You have to decide to desire it and then work at its cultivation.

God is the creator of all, including this wonderful communication form called music. The essence of musical sounds is found in the light spectrum. It is one of the most powerful elements of the Spirit of God created in the beginning of all things. Music is in the LIGHT spectrum and God is light. You have this same Creator residing in YOU.

I'm certain that we all have marveled at other people's artistic achievements and their insightful music ingenuity. Though that be true, there are vast deposits of songs and sounds awaiting your personal discovery. They can ultimately be released into the atmosphere if you'll fuel your desire and then cultivate them in the Holy Spirit's classroom of creativity. The world awaits the sound of believers singing a new song and a fresh retelling of the ageless story of God's Love. Start desiring, pressing inward, and create a fresh new sound.

God the Father has put a creative force in every man. Many unsaved ungodly people have created great works, the same even glorifying God. They were acknowledging God as best they understood Him. Volumes of scores mentioning God, scripture and character attributes fill music schools and libraries. Many of these works have become famous in music literature.

But Heaven's intent was that mankind commune with Him and not some other false god. We all understand that this current age is filled with counterfeits especially in the arts. There are many new age ideas attempting to sneak into the church via music. The world's stepchild of entertainment has a distorted, fleshly, mirror of true anointed music. In all of your efforts to create, I encourage you to stay with the Word.

Here's a simple one line thought to learn. It focuses your attention to the Father God, who is the original Creator of all.

God is the Creator—satan is the "peverter."

Let me repeat that and this time you say it so your ears hear it.

God is the Creator—satan is the "peverter."

Music was designed from the foundation of the world as a heavenly language between spirit beings. Its authentic function has always been to magnify and exalt God the Father. Scripture tells, "Thou art worthy, O Lord, to receive glory and honour and power: for thou hast created all things, and for thy pleasure they are and were created. (Revelation 4:11 KJV) The Amplified Bible says it this way, "Worthy are You, our Lord and God, to receive the glory and the honor and dominion, for You created all things; by Your will they were [brought into being] and were created. " As I've stated, the creative process is a very broad subject matter, so I will relieve you of some of its vastness by directing your focus to only a few key elements. These require your practical attention.

There is a level of responsibility that comes with the truth that God has put a creative force in every person. In reality, to be creative is to be Godlike. Some religious folk get very upset when it's taught that man is Godlike. They want to stay in an "old-sinner-saved-by-grace, I'm not worthy" mentality. Well, that's not Bible nor is it the heart of God! When you and I come into the Kingdom of God, are born again and fully restored in righteousness, our benefit package is full of great things. It contains giftings, Heavenly plans, assignments, dreams, songs, and more than we could ever ask. He fully is expecting for us to excel in our ability to influence the world with the Gospel, creatively, in our own unique style.

NATURE OF MUSIC

Now here's an underlying thought about music and your responsibility to make it excel. Turn this toggle switch on in your brain. Apply it to everything you create, because it will help you become more responsible and accountable of this powerful creative force. Fire has a nature. It BURNS. It can heat your house or burn it down. It doesn't care which it does. It just knows to burn. It demands proper attention or it could even burn your own city.

Music has a similar nature intrinsic in its DNA. By and large, it magnifies and exalts whatever it's put under. Let's see if you know these old commercial lyrics, "You deserve a break today at _____? " Here's a hint—a hamburger joint. Did you get it? How do you know that? Because for years McDonalds has played that phrase over and over on radio, TV and written text in print ads. You didn't have to go buy the recording. The musical soundtrack for the commercial simply magnified and exalted hamburgers, and may even have convinced you that you need to take a break today. So as you compose, remember that you are authorizing your words to be imprinted and magnified in the hearts of the hearer. Once penned, those lyrics will continually exalt whatever their content contains, long after you've left Planet Earth. Let everything you create exalt the fabric of the Word and its unconditional position of Love for all mankind through Jesus.

The tool of music is one of the strongest forces that has been misused and perverted by the enemy of our souls. The nature of that ex-worship leader satan is perversion, destruction, and lies. Christian musicians/artists must direct music's energy and focus to the Father, certainly not some squirrely, dumb, religious thought. Let it glorify God and something of His creation, His Love, His Word and all that's in it. Even let it tell a parable, a story, just as Jesus did to illustrate a point. J.S. Bach said it this way, "The aim and final end of all music should be none other than the glory of God and the refreshment of the soul."[16]

Here's another musical theological adjustment. I've heard my friend, anointed jazz pianist Ben Tankard, share this and it bears repeating. The sound of an A pitch note (A4) on the piano, guitar or even sung doesn't know if it's saved or not. It's not. It is neutral in its effort to vibrate on its own. I believe that note re-entering the atmosphere is awaiting your instruction. The vessel (you) and the sound (sung or played) released, determine its intent and its direction. Remember in Chapter 1, *Develop* Faithfulness, we established your image of being a vessel of honor. Those new notes through your fingers, your lips and heart create the direction of glory and honor.

MEDIATION IS THE MATRIX OF CREATIVITY

Matrix- It is the enclosure within which something originates or develops (from the Latin for womb).[17]

Meditation is the supply source for excelling in creativity. It's amazing that the more Word you put in, the Holy Spirit brings good, fresh things out in song or progressions. Meditation is not a new age term, although its function has been sorely mis-used by new age ideology. It's good to remind ourselves that meditation in nothing is still—nothing. Your mind may have settled down, but whatever is in your heart will bring forth its fruit. Meditation is not about humming some "ommmmm" sound that adjusts your alignment, whacky neurons and molecules.

---

[16] 2011, www.thinkexist.com/quotation
[17] 2011, www.audioenglish.net/dictionary

Godly meditation in and on the Word will always bring wonderful results. Although we've previously looked at this scripture, let's review it again in the context of meditation. After Moses death, Joshua is setting God's guideline for the future, "This book of the law shall not depart out of thy mouth; but thou shalt meditate therein day and night, that thou mayest observe to do according to all that is written therein: for then thou shalt make thy way prosperous, and then thou shalt have good success." (Joshua 1:8 KJV) David understood this real life principle and declared that we should be delighting in the Word. Remember, David is the "sweet psalmist" of Israel. "Blessed is the man that walketh not in the counsel of the ungodly, nor standeth in the way of sinners, nor sitteth in the seat of the scornful. But his delight is in the law of the LORD; and in his law doth he **meditate day and night.**" (Psalm 1:1-2 KJV)

The New Testament church grew in its ability to communicate in this creative language. Paul encouraged the church to exploit the process as he wrote a partner letter to the Body of Christ at Colossae. After all, Paul, along with his sidekick Silas, is famous for singing late night jailhouse songs that really set captives free! The songs the two of them sang were earth shattering. Paul was certainly a creative worshipper.

> "Let the word of Christ dwell in you richly in all wisdom; teaching and admonishing one another in **Psalms, and hymns and spiritual songs**, singing with grace in your hearts to the Lord. And whatsoever ye do in word or deed, do all in the name of the Lord Jesus, giving thanks to God and the Father by him." (Colossians 3:16-17 KJV)

Notice that Paul said that the Word of Christ dwelling in a believer should result in some teaching and admonishing utilizing (1) Psalms, (2) hymns, and (3) spiritual songs. Meditating on the Word causes creativity musically which will aid in instruction. I believe the more you sincerely press into the real source of Kingdom Light, you begin to have an unending reservoir of ideas. This does not mean that you'll turn into a KJV version of a Bible salesman. God always takes what He is given and expands and uses that gift as far as you're willing to stretch.

Many times, though, songs are written with only a semi-religious idea that sounds God-like, but isn't. Since we're given the privilege and responsibility of releasing faith filled life words into the atmosphere, we should be honorable to our craft. Have musical and spiritual integrity in your craft and life words in your songs. Give it a musical platform that reaches into dry places and refreshes others. Your Bible has a myriad of stories, insights, and methods given by a host of believers who love the same God that you desire to bless. This part of creation should certainly be ministry to God, not just for God.

Consider this truth about music in general. It exists in all of creation. Obviously, when mankind celebrates there's going to be some music involved. The art of creating music by man is first mentioned in the Bible in Genesis 4:21 when it speaks of Jubal, the father of all who handled the harp and organ. Early on, creation of most music stayed predominately inside the context of tabernacle worship. Leadership knew of music's extreme importance. David instituted a whole music academic system, including over four thousand priests who, "...praised the LORD with the instruments which I made, said David, to praise therewith." (1 Chronicles 23:5 KJV) In the MESSAGE BIBLE we discover that these singers and musicians, "...were well-trained in the sacred music, all of them masters." Instruction was given in the understanding of how to play, what to write, and how to do it all with excellence.

CULTIVATING CREATIVENESS

Here is another framework that will help your creativeness encompass excellence. I've been in full time music ministry unto the Lord, since I got saved in 1970. Having taught, performed, written, arranged, published and enjoyed many facets of musical usefulness in the Kingdom, I've come to a simplified formula that helps me understand the creative process and the various styles and functions of songs. The following chart helps me categorize music.

The following chart really has only one focus point for your ministry unto the Lord. Cultivate making **Great Music** that has practical, rock solid, **Excellent Theology**. Your songs should never insult God or have lyrics of doubt and unbelief. When you create a song that has excellence in its musical integrity along with well-crafted lyrics the song will live forever. That kind of song will transcend generations and may well be sung in Heaven. What do I mean?

Great Music with
Excellent Theology

Bad Music with Good Theology

Good Music with Bad Theology

Bad Music with Stupid Theology

Horrible Music with
Unintelligent Theology

Here's a classic example that contains excellence in music composition, as well as in its text. In Mid-August of 1741, George Frederick Handel finished his well-known oratorio entitled, *The Messiah,* in twenty-four days. His most famous portion, "Hallelujah Chorus" which is now performed predominantly at Christmas, was composed in just three days. *The Messiah* continues to be performed around the world and still has a powerful anointing on it and in it.

Although the ink dried in 1741 for this composition, it was joyfully revisited in 1992 with the result being *Handel's Messiah: A Soulful Celebration.*[18] This was a Grammy award winning Reprise Records concept album, performed by a choir of all-star gospel, contemporary Christian, R&B and jazz singers. The song was arranged and produced by Take 6 alumnus Mervyn Warren and conducted by Quincy Jones. It has the same impact as the original. *A Soulful Celebration* honors Jesus as King of Kings and Lord of Lords. The intensity of Handel's musical discipline is still producing excellence in creativity across many cultural genres.

This work has blessed countless of thousands of people for over 270 plus years. It demonstrates the truth that music is a very powerful

---

[18] 1992, "Handle's Messiah A Soulful Celebration", www.Wikipedia.org

spiritual force, especially when it's done with excellence and is anointed. The music that God helps you create may well have the same affect one day. Don't be slothful or lazy in cultivating creativeness. Be inventive in respect to the culture you live in.

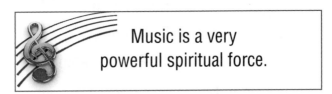

Music is a very
powerful spiritual force.

Here's another example. Around Christmas I saw several videos posted on YouTube of the *Silent Monks' Hallelujah Chorus*. The performers (not real monks) are dressed in long robes and head covers and stand in two rows holding placards. As the original recording of Handel's *The Messiah* plays, the monks hold up the appropriate cards to spell out the words to the chorus. The cards spell out HA-LE-LU-JAH. It's a humorous way this wonderful and exalting work still lives.

During the early days of ministering around the world teaching about the psalmist ministry, I would often give an assignment for the attending students. The task was for them to start writing their own original psalms, so as to stir up their creative thinking. We're not unlike David in our love for God and desire to worship. He wrote Psalms and so can we. David wasn't trying to write a hit to be sung everywhere. He just loved God, His mercy and righteousness, and wanted others to know about it. He did not have a musical scroll deal with a local Jerusalem music dealer to get his tunes on the iTalmud. He just wrote from his heart. Here's how one student responded to my assignment:

Psalm of Don

1. Praise you, Oh God for the ever refreshing assurance of your presence.
2. You speak to the depth of my being in the midst of the complexities of computers.

3. You know my heart that even as I watch a Bud Light commercial, I am reminded that you are my light and my salvation.
4. The tensions in the Persian Gulf do not leave me frightened.
5. The lying, cheating, killing by government, military, business and even religious leaders do not create a barrier between me and you, Oh God.
6. The knowledge of the evils of men coveting the oil in the bosom of your good earth shall not be satan's channel to steal my peace or lead me from being conscious of your presence.
7. I lift my hands in praise and open my heart to receive the rain of your blessings as you anoint me with your oil of healing and gladness.
8. As I behold the wonders of computers, I am even more convinced you know all about me and are aware of every detail of my past, present and future life.
9. How quickly, yea instantly, yea in the twinkling of an eye, can I erase what I have put on my McIntosh?
10. So quickly, so completely have you removed my sins from me.
11. And in the midst of the mind boggling capabilities of MIDI, I look unto You, the ALMIGHTY. Selah.[19]

The discipline of continually being creative has many outside enemies. Like all things where attention to detail is vital, you must find that special place or environment where it can work for you. Some song inspirations have come in a crowded restaurant or during a meeting.

I have written in all kinds of places. I've had song progressions come to me on airplanes and melodies show up in the middle of practicing scales. My wife Cheryl, who is a wonderful lyricist, had a new song birthed at a hotel while attending a Jerry Savelle meeting. Dr. Savelle was preaching about being a winner, not the loser or underdog. He made a statement about, "…never going under, but always going over." It was a victorious life giving message. The meeting ended with Dr. Jerry leading everyone in a victorious confession. It was awesome. Then He

---

[19] 1987, Don Bartow, "Psalm of Don," www.totallivingcenter.org

closed by saying, "We ain't never going under. We're always going over!" The next thing I heard from his voice was, "Steve …Cheryl… you have a song of the Lord. Come up here and sing it." Well, this is not the time to run to the car for a sound track. You can't grab a hymnal from the pew! That song isn't in a hymnal, but it is in us. This is when you have to get up and draw from inside your creative spirit-man. All of the preaching suddenly was boiled down to a simple four bar phrase that I got up and began to play. Cheryl grabbed a melody from the progression using those same words. "We ain't never going under. We're makin' plans for going over—Oh—Oh—Over—I'm talkin' about over—We ain't never goin' under—No!" The crowd exploded with rejoicing. The music had captured what the minister preached. The song was the exclamation mark. We later recorded "Never Going Under" on Cheryl's CD entitled, *All to You.*[20]

I share that to encourage you. The creative process is like the kitchen of your spirit man. You can get all the single individual ingredients together, which by themselves, don't seem like much. In a natural kitchen you know that a little cooking oil, raw eggs, baking soda and flour and sugar don't taste good individually, but all these ingredients mixed together can make a wonderful cake. Your practice, your learning scales and fingering, your work at singing and pitch all come together to produce a song. Excellence is always found in the details.

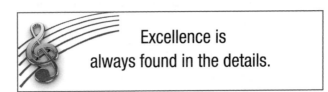

Excellence is always found in the details.

AREAS OF CREATIVITY

Another important ingredient is to study the various styles of music. Your knowledge of the carrier of lyrics and how to perform them can be a wonderful asset. If you are an instrumentalist, this may require

---

[20]1994© IMI Records, www.woffc.tv

some outside instruction to stretch your abilities. Maybe your style is black gospel with those nice fat chords and all the extra notes that sound so good. If that is your preference, I suggest that you be creative and investigate other arrangements of the same song. Train your ears and hands to grow some. Take the song into another key and style. Move it into a straight rock sound. This is just a suggestion to stir the creative juices so that your music communicates its message to more individuals.

Cheryl and I live in Florida where it's tropical and rarely cold. We like the sun, sand and the hint of the islands with some conch fritters. During our praise and worship expression, occasionally we will take a regular praise song and do it in a reggae type groove. It just brightens up the room and puts a "don't worry be happy" smile on everyone's face. Then there have been times when we change the color of a song by ending it with a pipe organ sound underneath the majestic ensemble and choir. My background was good old southern Baptist and hymns were always a staple part of our services.

Here's another observation. Machines don't write songs. People do. Computers and digital devices are aids to musical creation, but the creative genius of God is in man first and foremost. For sure, you and I will never let a silicon rock write our songs. Most songs have a whole set of human circumstances or stories tied to their creation. The motivation for creating comes from life experiences. We are God-like, therefore we praise and worship something or someone.

In the 18th and 19th centuries, hymns were the standard musical form in most churches worldwide. With the various spiritual renewals of evangelists such as the Wesley brothers, D.L. Moody, and Ira Sankey, there was an ever present need for good, solid Bible songs. Do you recognize any of these song titles? *Blessed Assurance, Pass Me Not O Gentle Saviour, Jesus Is Tenderly Calling You Home, Praise Him Praise Him, Rescue the Perishing,* and *To God Be the Glory?* These are but six of over 8,000 songs penned by a young lady whose father died during her first year. At just six weeks old, she caught a cold and had inflammation in her eyes, which caused her to lose her eyesight completely. She was raised by her mother and grandmother who never let her disability impede her creativity. Her life story is amazing and inspirational. She sold over 100 million copies of songs and is known as the "Queen of Gospel song writers," and as the "Mother of modern congregational singing in America." Her name is Frances Jane Crosby, or Fanny Crosby.[21]

In 1738, Charles Wesley suffered from pleurisy and was very doubtful about his own personal faith. After a short visit by some loving Christians who stirred his heart, he again pressed into God and made peace. He soon gloriously recovered. A year later on the anniversary of his healing and rededication he wrote an eighteen stanza hymn of which the seventh verse reads, *O For a Thousand Tongues to Sing*. He is known for publishing over 6,000 hymns. Charles Wesley wrote because he desired to bless the Kingdom of God. So can YOU. Allow the Creator to flow through you.

Some years ago, I became intrigued with wonderful possibilities of using a digital keyboard as an orchestrating device, and so invested in several racks of modules and keyboards. In my meditation time while reading various scriptures, I would wonder, "What would that scripture look and sound like if I were to see it in real life?" For example, I began to picture in my mind the scene of the mad demoniac nudist Jesus delivered. The story is found in Mark 5:1-20.

Jesus had delivered him from years of demonic possession. Suddenly he's in his right mind and wants to stay in this atmosphere with the Lord, but Jesus told him, "Go home and tell everyone the great things that God has done." I imagined this man, maybe in his Mid-40s, walking down that long dusty road back towards home. He's a bit reflective at first, wondering whether the family will accept him. Every now and then he'd twirl and start rejoicing all over again. As these pictures came to my mind, it gave me a wonderful rhythmic pattern. I created an unusual squish sound for his feet coupled with several odd percussion sounds. Then I arranged a melody played by a fat analog synth sound. It became a part of my musical trilogy entitled *Sounds of Love, Sounds of Joy* and *Sounds of Peace*. The song is called, "Back Home."

---

[21]2011, en.wikipedia.org

PREPARATION FOR CREATIVITY

Preparation time is never wasted time. I have taught this principle to musicians/psalmists in many countries. It is the practical homework assignment for cultivating creativeness and requires your investment of time and attention. Listed here are six areas to consider:

1. What do I prepare?—Great lyrics are the basis for a great song. Write something daily. Every good songwriter I know keeps a notebook full of ideas, phrases and song titles. Don't just mimic a KJV verse and think it will always work. Study word rhyming and word pictures. Try to tell the story with fewer words. As an instrumentalist, learn to play in all keys. Don't depend on a transpose button or guitar capo. Grow in your music theory. Study how to make chords and the various voicing of chords. Next, learn basic chord progressions and then play them in every key. Since there is an openness and reception of more contemporary styles and genres of music in many churches today, work on knowing how to play a song in as many styles as is useful to your pastor. Creativity can be hampered when all you know is one style of playing. We'll discuss this more in Chapter Six *Develop* Skillfulness.

2. Prepare your heart—Surely you know that the Holy Spirit loves to be entreated and invited to join you. Get rid of distractions and people situations. Stay out of strife. It's not creatively productive to be angry at everybody and then try to create a song of God's unconditional Love. Enjoy what you're doing and make room for intimate fellowship with the Creator. It pays great dividends to just enjoy being with the Father.

3. Prepare to study—2 Timothy 2:15 in THE MESSAGE Bible declares that we should, "Concentrate on doing your best for God, work you won't be ashamed of, laying out the truth plain and simple." Read great song lyrics. Get a repertoire of hymns and study them, all the verses. Listen to how songs are arranged and built. Invest more time and effort in detailed study of songs, their voicings and arrangements.

4. Prepare to rewrite—Occasionally, writers are not flexible enough. I suggest you not become too protective and rigid of your song creation that you may miss a greater rewrite. Ask yourself; is this finished product my best? A song should have all the components such as a memorable melody and a good hook. The hook grabs the hearer and pulls them in. Does your song stay within correct stanzas of poetry and musical notation? Does your creation have all the necessary ingredients for a great cake? Your kitchen should smell great with all the creative excitement and anticipation in your song.

5. Prepare in the Spirit—As you pray and sing in the Spirit you are stirring up your, "…most holy faith…" (Jude 1:20 KJV) This also clears the atmosphere where you're working. Cheryl and I have known of great songs that came from rehearsal sessions. Whether alone or working with a team of musicians and singers, we recommend learning to flow musically out of your spirit. What a fabulous way to develop trusting relationships socially and musically. The Father loves it too.

6. Prepare to bless others—The world treats its musical heroes as gods. They are mistakenly allowed to be eccentric and often unkind to others. Unfortunately, success in certain arenas causes some to have an elevated opinion of their abilities and persona. You and I are members of the Body of Christ. We're all on the same winning team. There is no place for self-worship in God's Kingdom. Musicians should become generous with other novices or beginning students. You benefit from giving to others and aiding them in their craft.

OTHER ATTRIBUTES OF MUSIC

I have mentioned the nature of music is to exalt and magnify. This is its primary function; however there are many other attributes that creative music can produce. A wonderful component of music's ability is to speak all kinds of languages.

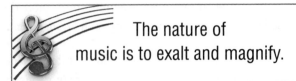

The nature of music is to exalt and magnify.

Creative music can comfort, minister, and produce great joy. It can destroy burdens. It certainly can heal. It has the ability to excite people and to evangelize. It can cause people to unite, and it will do mighty warfare. As you continue to grow in your excellence in music ministry, broaden your arsenal of music and spiritual tools to include all of these elements.

Stay mindful of the condition of your heart in this too. Flood your inner man and heart with His Word, particularly the messages taught by your pastor. After all, he is YOUR shepherd sent by God to watch over your life. He is feeding you a good meal every week. Our loser enemy will never be your source. The World will not be your source. As your mind and heart grows, God will use your gift and creativeness in song to bless your place of worship. It is in the safety of the house of God that your creativeness can really flourish.

Live with this evidence of which I have inserted some language of creative liberty for emphasis, "The upright (honorable, intrinsically good) man **[Psalmist]** out of the good treasure [*stored*] in his heart produces **[sounds and songs]** that are upright (honorable and intrinsically good), and the evil man out of the evil storehouse brings forth that which is depraved (wicked and intrinsically evil); for out of the abundance (overflow) of the heart **[of a Psalmist]** his mouth speaks. (Luke 6:45 AMP)

Cultivate creativeness …the kitchen is open.

CHAPTER SEVEN

DEVELOP SKILLFULNESS

The quality of skillfulness in any endeavor is a never ending process of a desired disciplined delight. I say that not esoterically, but specifically, as the basic method to obtaining the necessary parts that produce excellence of ministry. I call this endeavor the *Three D* method. You take your absolute red hot **desire,** you go through some Godly **discipline,** and it will become an awesome **delight!** I'll share more about that later.

Pause a moment and meditate on the following quotes in regard to pursuing your goal. The famous Green Bay Packers coach, Vince Lombardi, welded these powerful words into his team members on the football field and made champions out of mediocre players, "The quality of a person's life is in direct proportion to their commitment to excellence, regardless of their chosen field of endeavor. The difference between a successful person and others is not a lack of strength, not a lack of knowledge, but rather in a lack of will."[22]

There's an anecdotal story of the famed Spanish composer/cellist, Pablo Casals, about his commitment to developing skill. A young reporter asked him, "Mr. Casals, you are ninety-five years old and the greatest cellist that ever lived. Why do you still practice six hours a day?" The humble cellist responded, "Because I think I'm making progress."

---

[22]2011, www.vincelombardi.com/quotes

Since your goal is excellence in music ministry, with the emphasis on music, for the moment, let's look at a historic rock and roller, the shepherd boy, David. You know the Sunday school Bible stories of his protecting the sheep for dad and having to kill lions, tigers and bears. Oh my. You know something about his amazing trip out to the battle field to carry some peanut butter and jelly sandwiches to his brothers and his ultimate encounter with the giant, Goliath. David caused a riot and Goliath lost his head that day. You've heard the story of King David leading the historic parade returning the Ark of the Covenant to Jerusalem and his outrageous rendition of Motown's, *Dancing in the Streets,* before Martha and the Vandellas even recorded it.

I've always been intrigued by the wonderful scriptures that describe David. With the Book of Psalms, he became the largest contributor to the school of music for the Kingdom of God. These next references are a foundation for you today and your commitment of excellence in developing skill in your craft. Look at these verses,

> "He **chose** David His servant and took him from the sheep-folds…" (Psalm 78:70 KJV)
> "Then Samuel took the horn of oil, and anointed him in the midst of his brethren: and the Spirit of the LORD came upon David from that day forward. So Samuel rose up, and went to Ramah." (1 Samuel 16:13 KJV)
> "Then answered one of the servants, and said, Behold, I have seen a son of Jesse the Bethlehemite, *that is* **cunning in playing**, and a mighty valiant man, and a man of war, and prudent in matters, and a comely person, and the LORD *is* with him." (1 Samuel 16:18 KJV)

The Amplified version of 1 Samuel 16:18 reads,

> "One of the young men said, I have seen a son of Jesse the Bethlehemite who **plays skillfully,** a valiant man, a man of war, prudent in speech and eloquent, an attractive person; and the Lord is with him."

Note the way scripture describes several elements of his character. First of all, they knew that he played skillfully. Evidently his musical reputation was widespread. King Saul's high court staff even knew about him and his music. And it's apparent they knew that he was valiant, had great warring abilities, and could communicate well. If that wasn't enough, he was an attractive, good looking young man and—here's the best—the Lord was with Him. People recognized that an anointing rested on him.

You may be saying, "So what? That's not me! I don't play well. I'm a bit shy and …" Excuses. Well I don't know about all your reasons for not growing musically, but I do know that ever since I became a believer, things have changed for the better. I know that the anointing in and on my life has made the difference, and I'm working on all the other elements that I can change. I'm determined to grow into all of that. I do know you can develop skillfulness. It will take a change of your attitude and mindset. My ministry friend, Pastor Clyde Oliver, is always reminding people, "God has great plans for you and none of them include defeat!" Adopt that attitude about your life and ministry.

How did David become such a skilled musician? How did he learn warfare at such an early age? And how did all these other attributes display themselves? Let's consider a few of them and draw some parallels. Becoming skillful is not out of your reach, regardless of age, education or even where you live. God will meet you right where you are.

The scriptures mention that David was skillful. Developing skill requires a plan of simple sets of exercises that, once learned, become automatic and natural to your growth. These exercises give your fingers, or voice, the ability of performing one note following another in tune and in time. I believe that David took his little lute guitar looking instrument to the hillside as he watched and guarded his dad's sheep. He was obedient first to do what Dad asked. He showed up to tend the sheep daily, habitually. It baffles me that some folk want the platform or the microphone, but won't show up for rehearsal or show up late. What about you? Are you being obedient to the Father? While he was there day and night, he would compose and play songs to those sheep, trying new melodies and rhythms at his pleasure. Responding to the beautiful night scenes that he described later in Psalm Eight, he continuously serenaded the sheep. The animals had no opinion whether or not it sounded good. Their concern was being well loved and cared for. He would give it his all, sometimes somber and soothing and then other times outrageously clamorously foolish! Stretch your imagination with me. To the naked eye, he only had the visible audience of those sheep, some goats, and some wolves lurking around. In his eyes and heart, however, he had the glorious spectacular heavenly hosts of Jehovah God as his audience. WOW!

David used the time element of honoring his father's assignment as a classroom study in developing skill. He used the *Three D Method*. I believe that just like David, you can take your Godly desire, go through some disciplined efforts in respect to your craft (instrument or vocal), and you can become full of Godly delight. It worked for David and our God is no respecter of persons.[23] In truth, this powerful psalmist told on himself, "Delight yourself also in Jehovah, and He shall give you the desires of your heart." (Psalm 37:4 KJV) Being on the mountainside with sheep became a delightful place of developing skill in the Lord. Is that too simple? Not really.

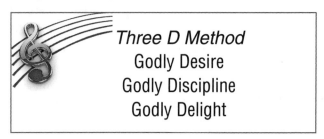

Three D Method
Godly Desire
Godly Discipline
Godly Delight

Remember that the Word gives more than one attribute of David. Look again at his description; (1) he plays skillfully, (2) he is a valiant man, (3) he is a man of war, (4) he is prudent in speech, (5) he is eloquent, (6) he is an attractive person and, (7) the Lord is with him. This man of God with all of his bumps, flaws and mistakes had a heart for God and refused to become religious. When he made mistakes or wrong decisions, he quickly repented and never made those again. He

---

[23]Scripture reference — Acts 10:34

wanted to please God. He desired and obtained a relationship in God that permeated all of his life including his leadership skills. His heart for God was on such display that he attracted the recognition of being known worldwide as "the sweet psalmist of Israel." (2 Samuel 23:1 KJV) Later when he had become King, he put into motion a method of servant leadership with great attention to worship detail as no other had done. His covenant relationship with God dictated from his perspective that people love God and make sacrifices from their hearts. Therefore with his skill set of leading people with wisdom, requiring sacrifices of praise and never quitting or being faint of heart, King David developed an intense school of music for the tabernacle.

His training program and guidelines were specific and detailed. You should do your own study about this. Here are a few insightful scriptures for the framework of developing skillfulness.

"And these are they whom David set over the **service of song** in the house of the LORD, after that the ark had rest." (1 Chronicles 6:31 KJV)

"And they ministered before the dwelling place of the tabernacle of the congregation with singing, until Solomon had built the house of the LORD in Jerusalem: and then they waited on their office according to their order." (1 Chronicles 6:32 KJV)

"And David spake to the chief of the Levites to appoint their brethren to be the singers with instruments of musick, psalteries and harps and cymbals, sounding, by lifting up the voice with joy." (1 Chronicles 15:16 KJV)

"So the singers, Heman, Asaph, and Ethan, *were appointed* to sound with cymbals of brass…" (1 Chronicles 15:19 KJV)

"And Zechariah, and Aziel, and Shemiramoth, and Jehiel, and Unni, and Eliab, and Maaseiah, and Benaiah, with psalteries on Alamoth…" (1 Chronicles 15:20 KJV)

"And Mattithiah, and Elipheleh, and Mikneiah, and Obededom, and Jeiel, and Azaziah, with harps on the Sheminith to excel." (1 Chronicles 15:21 KJV)

"And Chenaniah, chief of the Levites, *was* for song: he instructed about the song, because he *was* skilful." (1 Chronicles 15:22 KJV)

Note several things through these short verses. David ordered for music to serve and to be done with joy. He chose musicians who excelled and were skillful. This is but a few words of insightful encouragement from a King who got God's attention and established the best. I believe that coupled with your own Bible study, your quality decision to grow, as well as your faithfulness to become excellent in your craft, you can experience a new dimension in anointed praise and worship in houses of God all around the world. Somebody say Amen!

How do you develop in this area of music ministry excellence? All music, regardless of style, can be broken down into smaller pieces. For example as a vocalist or instrumentalist, the essence of music has to do with scales. We derive most melodies from scales. You can begin daily tithing your time in preparation of a ministry of excellence. Determine to learn several scales every day. Sing them in tune. Play them with correct fingering and timing. Vocalists need to have breathing exercises that aid pitch and stamina. (See Recommended Resources) As a guitarist, you may need to learn more scales and chords so that you can broaden your range. As you rehearse and stretch yourself, let it also become a time of joy and worship. Warm-ups can become a sacrifice of praise.

Another area of discipline musically is to learn a wide degree of styles of music. Vocally this may mean that you challenge yourself to sing with no vibrato or learn to blend your voice with others. Work on the color or tone of your voice and for certain learn to sing in tune. Likewise pianists, keyboardists and guitarists need to expand music styles so you can have a wider variety of resources. Soloists should discipline themselves musically to become uniquely skilled. The important issue is to give God something to work with. Show yourself faithful where you are and with what you're given.

Another element in this regard is to do these exercises all unto the Lord. Make it fun and allow the spirit of praise and worship to flow. Years ago, one of my mentors in learning spirit music, trumpeter/psalmist Phil Driscoll, suggested that you should open the Book of Psalms and dig deep in your spirit for a melody to place the words on. He'd open the Word and just start playing a groove and then sing, "Well the Word says here to…" and he'd sing whatever psalm he was in. Learning to practice and worship with scales, chords, and new keys is really fun. Your level of confidence can increase immensely.

Let's say you've learned your favorite song on the keyboard or guitar. You're very good with that song and could play it blindfolded. Assign yourself homework. Take your time and transpose up a half or whole step. Learn to perform your music in several keys. Maybe even go a fourth up the scale. Why? You will find that more music theory is getting into your head, as well as more chords and voicings. That's a good thing.

In regard to music theory here are a few thoughts. It's a truth that while some resist the discipline, learning to read music will, in fact, teach you more about theory and music. It won't hurt you're playing but will actually enhance it. Smile. Here's a simplistic question.

Somewhere in your past you learned to read the words cat…dog… Jack…Jill. It hasn't hurt your speaking, has it? You learned to read. It took some time, and I'm glad you read now so that I can minister to you through this book. Get rid of a bias that written music isn't hip or necessary. Go ahead and learn to read chord charts, notes, and enjoy more music. Stop with the excuse, "Do I have to learn to read?" No you don't, but it expands your abilities, especially in working with others.

Ear training is another important element in music ministry. It's almost on the other end of the spectrum from reading music. Both are extremely important for a ministry of excellence. If this is lacking, discipline yourself to begin training your ears. As a keyboardist and psalmist, I pressed for help from the Holy Ghost to learn to recognize chord progressions and their repetition. While traveling, I often listen to various styles of music, focusing on the bass line and the changes it makes. Generally the progression of the song can be predicted, because of the cyclical nature of most songs. Chord progressions will often follow a circle of fours and/or fives. Once you develop your ear to hear them, you're in another league of quality players. It becomes a real treat to hear one verse or chorus of a song and then join in playing without the aid of a score.

The internet has innumerable online resources in regard to musical education and songs. Some web sites will provide music lessons often for free. You only have to register and occasionally endure some annoying advertisements. You can gain immediate insight to many current praise and worship songs via various YouTube postings of instructional videos. Maybe your ears aren't quite capturing a chord progression or voicing. Many times by observing someone else play you can quickly learn the song. Although some YouTube postings are amateurish, many are quite instructional. Major publishers and record labels have sites with available downloadable lyrics, scores, and chord charts for a small fee. You can also get full scores for orchestra parts. The internet is a deep reservoir of information and insights for psalmists.

In regard to rehearsals for choir and musicians, each church sets its agenda, standards, and guidelines. In general, musicians should rehearse separately and be well prepared before adding vocals to the rehearsal. Likewise, vocals should be separately rehearsed and prepared to join the musicians later. Rehearse privately. Never do a public rehearsal just before a service. It is unacceptable in my mind for musicians to walk in and try to learn songs in front of a congregation who they are going to try to lead in worship. Private rehearsals are necessary so that teamwork mentality can be established.

Vocalists need the uninterrupted time of learning parts and blend without the annoyance of musicians noodling. Vocalists must learn to blend the color and tone of voices as well as pitch or tuning of chords and parts. Just for example, we currently do a mid-week rehearsal of vocal ensemble and choir. We begin with prayer, and then have musical warm-ups, utilizing *Vocal Aerobics,* by Steve Bowersox.[24] Then we work on material for upcoming services. Lyric sheets and other resources such as rehearsal CD's or web links are available. Our routine is to do an early Sunday morning sound check/rehearsal for the audio team and musicians, going over the song list for that service. Since the sound check is held in the auditorium, it is closed to the public and held an hour and half before service time. We add

---

[24] 2011, Steve Bowersox,"Vocal Aerobics," www.BowersoxInstitute.com

the vocal ensemble and choir thirty minutes later, adjusting monitor/ audio levels. This early sound check/rehearsal gives opportunity to change songs or make key adjustments if necessary. After prayer the sanctuary is opened thirty minutes before service with appropriate music and videos playing. This allows the musicians and singers to have quality time to get their spirits ready to minister to the Father and to the people. Last minute rehearsing should never occur before ushering in the presence of God.

Regardless of how you develop your skills, instrumentally or vocally, give it your best. Maybe for the moment you can only start with some free internet lessons, or watch videos, or learn from some friends. Whatever you do, give it your best. I believe that with some Holy Spirit led prayer and discipline you can accomplish great musical value for the Kingdom of God. Keep your standard high. Play in time and sing in tune! Develop skill. Believe God for the investment costs and do it right. Private lessons will aid in your accountability. Having to meet with a mentor or coach will increase your discipline. The key is to begin a schedule that will result in consistency. Set your goals on paper and give yourself a measurable timetable that is realistic.

I remind you again. Every musician or singer needs to take the commitment that ninety-five year old Pablo Casals had on practicing. You keep doing it because you think you're seeing progress. All in all it's important that you prove yourself, and prove to yourself, that you are a psalmist, a vessel of honor—prepared to do every good work—a skilled singer/musician. Now go back out to the hillside and crank up some development of more skill. The sheep are waiting and will be very glad to hear you. They really do enjoy you.

CHAPTER EIGHT

ESTABLISH PURPOSE

The Apostle Paul wrote in his letter to the church at Colossae, "And say to Archippus, take heed to the ministry which thou hast received in the Lord, that thou fulfil it." (Colossians 4:17 KJV) It is imperative that you complete your calling. The Body of Christ is depending on your faithful obedience.

This book's intention is to develop healthy, creative vessels of honor, intent on completing their course and eventually hearing, "Well done my good and faithful servant." Upon your arrival in Heaven, you don't want to hear the Lord say to you, "Well....?" It is essential that you keep the Father's purpose in your mind—the harvest—souls—the influence in this world for His Name and the maturing of the Body of Christ. Ministry to people comes first before attention to your latest CD or project. What a tragedy if you had studied, worked hard, and increased in various areas only to discover you were pressing for the wrong goal. I know people want to applaud you and your abilities, but you must maintain Godly humility. What a waste of potential for you to get wrapped up in the same kind of hype about music that the world does. What a waste of true influence if we personally take the credit. A minister of excellence is able to maintain a balance in all of these areas.

I remember ministering in a world conference in Nassau, Bahamas, and listening to the powerful ministry of Dr. Myles Munroe. He was teaching the wonderful truth that God had us in mind before the foundation of the world.[25] God starts with the end and then starts.[26] He calls things that aren't as though they were.[27] We are the ones He wanted, and He planned to redeem us before the foundation of the world. He watched the whole movie of the world before the film was in the camera. Dr. Myles's teaching underscores what I've done many times as an arranger. Start with the end in mind.

Studio arrangers understand this. From my perspective, I start with a sound in mind and an idea of how I want the ending to be. While there are always adjustments, modulations, pauses etc., I know generally where we'll wind up at the coda. The arranger must consider the range of the singer, coupled with an intense study of the melody and lyric content. The latter gives knowledge of what has to be said and how long will it take. Obviously, adjustments are made for the vocalist who may surprise you as he/she becomes more motivated to stretch their vocal range. The goal is to make sure that the vocalist is comfortable and can perform it well.

I remember hearing the classic arrangement of the immortal Dottie Rambo song, *We Shall Behold Him*.[28] It was performed by Sandi Patti and arranged beautifully by David T. Clydesdale. With Sandi's enormous vocal span of four octaves, there was never a question about modulating one more time. The song demanded it.

Keep your focus on the purpose of your ministry of excellence. You will run your race of loving people with joy and resolve, introducing them to the majestic matchless grace of Jesus. Your focus should not be just winning a Grammy or Stellar award, but rather that your music is used as a major influence in the world. Heaven has a better reward system here and there. You know that it's His Name that changes lives, not you or your song performance.

Music ministry covers so many facets. For everyone, life in general creates musical influences. A wedding, a funeral, and a bar-mitzvah all have differing musical sounds. Each event requires a different musical

---

[25] Scripture reference — Matthew 25:34
[26] Scripture reference — Isaiah 46:10
[27] Scripture reference — Romans 4:17
[28] 1980, "We Shall Behold Him," © *John T. Benson Publishing*

format and style, but all of them serve the moment and the people in them. Too many churches today are fighting brainless theological worship wars about styles and function. Regardless of whether you're singing for a street ministry or a wedding, your inner joy should be to glorify God in every arena. Every time you minister, you should sense the anointing of God. Here are some thoughts for understanding where God has called you.

In the church music realm, there are three main arenas of music function; the Outer Court, the Inner Court, and the Holy of Holies. Many wonderful commentaries give great insights of Old Testament details on the facets of worship in the Tabernacle. I'm not dismissing their importance, but for our purpose, I want to simply use this as a reference point. I do believe, without reservation, that a minister of excellence should be able to function in all of these areas.

The Outer Court was in sight of all the people who would come and watch as the priest prepared to present himself to God. The Outer Court was also the place of praise where psalms were chanted proclaiming the glory of God. In today's culture, the equivalent would be evangelistic efforts. This musical endeavor is not, necessarily, inside the four walls of a church building. The musical style, with its message contained in lyrics, has more hooks and groove and is appealing to those who are accustomed to the genre.

Inner Court ministry is extremely important. In the first chamber of the Inner Court, the Holy Place, the priests kept a table of Shewbread,[29] representing the presence and Word of God. Today we would equate this as being the local church. Musicians in the church function as praise and worship leaders and the event is generally referred to as the worship service, whether worship happens or not. I don't mean that derogatorily, but as a point that real worship is very intimate and doesn't always have musical accompaniment. Intimacy is attainable, but people must seek after Him. Paul understood this position when he said, "Let the word of Christ dwell in you richly in all wisdom; teaching and admonishing one another in psalms and hymns and spiritual

---

[29] 2011, www.bible-history.com/tabernacle

songs, singing with grace in your hearts to the Lord." (Colossians 3:16 KJV) Paul instructed church members to be worshippers in all that they endeavored and to wait on God. That word "wait" means to "serve."[30] Praise and worship is our service to the Lord.

The Holy of Holies housed the Ark of the Covenant and was a sacred place reserved for closeness and intimacy with the Father God. Before David established the Tabernacle of David, [31]the Holy of Holies was separated from the people. Only the high priest could enter and then only one time of year to offer sacrifices for the people's sin. David placed the Ark where everyone could see that God is alive, and He is with us. This was a foreshadowing of what Christ ultimately accomplished. David's heart speaks, "One *thing* have I desired of the LORD, that will I seek after; that I may dwell in the house of the LORD all the days of my life, to behold the beauty of the LORD, and to enquire in his temple." (Psalm 27:4 KJV) Our heart's attitude is the source of entrance here, not talent and certainly not fame. "Who shall ascend into the hill of the LORD? or who shall stand in his holy place? He that hath clean hands, and a pure heart; who hath not lifted up his soul unto vanity, nor sworn deceitfully." (Psalm 24:3-4 KJV) The Holy of Holies should be a sought after place where time does not exist, and no one is in a hurry. In the secret place of the Holy of Holies, you discover a relationship with Almighty God and the purpose of your calling is unfolded.

Whether in the Outer Court, the Inner Court, or the Holy of Holies, time spent in true worship is vital. Cheryl and I have functioned for years in and out of all of three. We have been thrilled to stand before thousands outdoors, minister in prisons, and perform on secular television. We thoroughly enjoy contributing to a music service in a church setting with good musicians and singers. I have to say though, where I am most comfortable, and the place I sincerely welcome is to sit and worship at my keys. I soak in His presence with no song form or melody, but only the thought, "I glorify your Name Lord." Shhhhhh…

---

[30] 2011, www.bible.org/article/waiting
[31] 2011, www.enwikepedia.org/wiki/tabernacle

it gets so sweet, and there's so much Love and grace. What precious moments are there.

None of this happens without pressing in to fulfill our purpose. The Father is seeking those, "...that worship Him in spirit and in truth." (John 4:24 KJV) It's such a joy to know flow of the Holy Spirit and not worry about trying to build a career. Stay in your call and anointing. You could mention your favorite music ministers, and we'd all applaud them, but the single most important thing for you to weld and solidify in your spirit is that you must excel in being you in Christ. You may want to emulate someone, learn from their anointing, and even use their sound tracks, but you should press in to be the best **YOU** that you can be. I am amazed at the prolific writings and wonderful output of classic gospel music from psalmists like Andraé Crouch. Songs like, *The Blood*, *To God Be the Glory*, and *Through It All* have impacted nations. Precious Dottie Rambo was a prolific writer and worshipper with such a wonderful kind spirit. Although she now resides in Heaven, her songs remain with us. Heaven wants you to learn to write. Heaven wants you to excel. As a minister, I absolutely assure you that we all need and want you to grow because you provide something no one else can or ever will. Phil Driscoll, psalmist/trumpeter is awesome and a very wonderful example of a player of spirit music and power worship, but we need other horn players to pucker up and get their horns blowing. I could repeat this addendum a hundred more times, but you're getting the tune, I trust.

Establishing purpose requires setting some realistic goals, spiritually and musically. It is a process of time and the growth process is so important. Before you are promoted to a world stage, be faithful, honorable, and available in your local house of worship. God promotes, not on the basis of talent or charisma, but on one thing alone—your faithfulness and obedience.

The House of Ingram has always had a home church, a pastor and we have always tithed. Cheryl and I settled that before we married. We will be givers and tithers all the days of our lives here on earth. We've served many pastors in various ways. I remember when our musical group Alpenglow was birthed in Central Florida, and we received a recording contract with Housetop Records, a record company through

Pat Robertson's Christian Broadcasting Network. We were traveling doing concerts, Jesus festivals, churches, and performing on the *700 Club* television program once a month. What a time of intense ministry. We wore out three engines in our remodeled Trailways Silver Eagle bus. As busy as we were, we continued to attend, sing, and bless our local church in Winter Haven, Florida. We didn't sleep in on Sunday morning, because we had performed a concert in Tallahassee the night before. If we were home, we were in church. Before moving to Texas and working fulltime at KCM, the ministry would fly me out to the city where their meeting was. I would rehearse, play piano for Brother Copeland's three day believers meetings, play the closing song, *How Great Thou Art*, on Saturday night, catch a red-eye flight home, crawl into bed way past midnight, and get up early Sunday, so I could be in my place at the keyboard at church. What am I saying? Stay focused on the purpose of it all. You are in a wonderful company of faith fighters who are tearing down strongholds of the enemy and doing great exploits for the Kingdom of God!

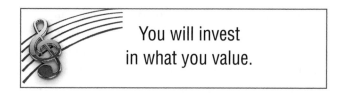

**You will invest
in what you value.**

Establish purpose by investing in others of like vision. You will invest in what you value. Every step of faith that Cheryl and I have taken in ministry has demanded that we sow significant seed and do it consistently. Bless those around you and over you in the Lord. These leaders are enduring real spiritual battles of warfare. Be sure to be a part of their answer and not their problem. They deserve an agreeable team spirit from you. Be a real team player running only the plays they are planning. When you're the coach, then you can lead.

If you're not aware yet, wake up! The territory we're all moving into and reclaiming has had a wimp, lying, renegade musician who has cleverly deceived thousands with the position of fame. You and I need to sow for a harvest into those generals, lieutenants, and leaders. Your money supply problem isn't the problem really. If God has given you direction and calling, then as Oral Roberts told Brother Copeland, "Get your job done at any cost," because if God told you to do it, then there will be a supply. Sow your time, sow physical support of participation, and sow finances.

Whether teaching, preaching or singing, I must make it clear again; this is always about souls—people who have no clue about God's gracious and generous needed gift of salvation through Jesus. The world thinks that they want to hear a song for some relief or amusement or entertainment. Most of the world's purpose of music is flesh—self. "Let's hook up. Let's get physical." The culture's view of music is demeaning to its purpose. You and I have the most awesome stealth tool in God's army—anointed excellent music. Let's major in music evangelism through the Outer Court. Create sounds and lyrics that captivate hearts and bring people to Jesus. Let's be ready in season and out of season to serve in the church in the Inner Court, and let's find that secret place of worship in the Holy of Holies.

CHAPTER NINE

DEMAND EXCELLENCE

Excellence is found in the details. Recall that I mentioned in Chapter Two *Open* Door, I was confronted with the spirit of excellence at summer music camp, and somewhere along this journey, discovered that details matter. I haven't arrived. I continue to be dissatisfied with where I am, so I continually strive for more. I want to be pleasing to the Father, and I so desire to remain teachable. The Holy Spirit will have it no other way. Through years of ministry, I've seen that putting the correct amount of effort makes the difference, particularly when you minimize the distractions and maximize your expectations. The Greek philosopher, Aristotle is quoted as saying, "We are what we repeatedly do. Excellence, then, is not an act, but a habit." [32] I treasure these "Colesisms"[33] by Dr. Ed Cole, "Mediocre men work at their best; men seeking excellence strive to do better," and "Excellence is not the ability to do something once, but to do it successively successfully."[34]

Present day society has seen a drastic dissolving of some of life's primary character attributes; integrity, morality and the spirit of excellence. The Kingdom of God has the only real and lasting answers and solutions, because the Kingdom inhabits God's own majestic, glorious

[32] 2011, www.brainyquote.com/quotes
[33] 2011, "Coleisms—the Ed Cole ® Library," www.edcole.org
[34] ibid

character. A minister of excellence can greatly reduce the distractions of this world by listening for the cheers coming from the grandstand of Heaven and the Father himself. "Do you see what this means—all these pioneers who blazed the way, all these veterans cheering us on?" (Hebrews 12:1 THE MESSAGE) You and I are here on earth for a brief whisper of time in regard to eternity. There is so much to learn, grow into and obtain. Even though the world tries to slow or impede you, there is still this truth—our God is more than able.

Let's reestablish a truth you should already know. We've seen this reference several times and it bears repeating in the Amplified Bible, "For I know the thoughts and plans that I have for you, says the Lord, thoughts and plans for welfare and peace and not for evil, to give you hope in your final outcome." (Jeremiah 29:11 AMP)

When God says the words "I know," then that should settle the "*if*" kind of question on whether you'll be a success. There is no maybe or hesitation when God says, "I know." You certainly understand. God has a ministry of excellence set aside for you and you must embrace it. You my friend must pursue it, sleep with it, dream about it, and ultimately fulfill it. Whew! In THE MESSAGE of that same scripture in Jeremiah, the words are magnified, "I know what I'm doing. I have it all planned out—plans to take care of you, not abandon you, plans to give you the future you hope for."(Jeremiah 29:11 THE MESSAGE)

To help you further, Paul spoke with great insight when He spoke to the charismatic church in Ephesus sharing an explosive truth,

> " [That you may really come] to know [practically, through experience *for yourselves*] the love of Christ, which far surpasses mere knowledge [without experience]; that you may be filled [through all your being] unto all the fullness of God [may have the richest measure of the divine Presence, and become a body wholly filled and flooded with God Himself]" "Now to Him Who, by (in consequence of) the [*action of His*] power that is at work within us, is able to [*carry out His purpose and*] do superabundantly, far over and above all that we [dare] ask or think [infinitely beyond our highest prayers, *desires, thoughts, hopes, or dreams*] To Him

be glory in the church and in Christ Jesus throughout all generations forever and ever. Amen (so be it)." (Ephesians 3:19-21 AMP)

This ought to light your fire, unless your wood is explicitly soaked with doubt and unbelief. Our God, whom you know through Jesus and His Word, is able to carry out His purpose and do superabundantly, far over, and above all that we dare ask or think. I don't know about you, but my creative imagination is pretty vast. That's wild! That tells me that there is no problem of manifesting excellence. It's not really God's responsibility either. He has made it available, and we must receive it, pay the price, and pursue it. I've heard this next statement preached often lately, and it puts me on alert every time. As startling as this might be to some, God has done all he is going to do! God has already given you a personal set of keys to your ministry. He will not insert the keys. He will not crank the engine nor put it in gear. He will not steer it, but He will guide you, if you'll listen. The Holy Spirit will run interference for you while Jesus intercedes and prays for you. He'll bless every bit of the resources that you sow from your heart. He is the High Priest over the tithe. You have to make the quality decision, this can and will be manifest in my life.

The use of the word demand is not meant to be harsh, but rather an encouragement. You must grasp its essence with boldness and resolve. Place a demand on your time, your energy, but most of all, your decision to do it. Brother Copeland has taught for years the term *quality decision* is one in which there is no retreat. It is a healthy, encouraging, decision to step up to a higher level of ministry and influence. Be watchful that the spirit of the Laodiceans[35] doesn't find a comfort spot in you or your church today. A Laodicean attitude is neither faithful nor unbelieving, but rather it causes people to be utterly indifferent. People then possess a self-satisfied mentality in which they think everything is fine. You cannot afford one moment of that devilish attitude that will leave you defeated, never seeing the victory God has for you.

---

[35] Scripture reference — Revelation 3:14-16

Except for the underground persecuted church, it appears that many have had it too easy or have been slack or self-centered in their efforts. I've traveled around the world and seen just about every kind of worship service and expression you could imagine. The rare commodity of a pursuit of excellence is not yet the norm. I sense though that there's a radical new breed of believers who want the real and anointed rather than the counterfeit and puffed up. Real hunger for God will always compel real believers. That's why I say that you should demand excellence of yourself. I pray and agree you'll approach that quality decision just within days and hours of reading this.

I believe and confess that this resource of excellence in music ministry can continue to bless, encourage, and be a roadmap for you to fulfill God's call and Heaven's plan. You are desirable and have been prayed for by Jesus.[36] You have a useful gift that will bless thousands that I'll never meet till we gather in Heaven. I've ministered for years about completing your destiny in a message entitled, *Don't Go to Your Grave with Your Music Still in You.* I encourage you to accomplish what God originally put you here for. Regardless of when you start, at least start or restart! It only takes a little extra energy to move into excellence.

Here's a non-musical example for demanding excellence. We all know that hot water will burn your skin. Scientists tell us water can do great damage at 211degrees. At 212 degrees it begins to boil as a conversion takes place. The difference of that small one degree is tremendous. It will begin to produce steam, which when collected, can move and do mighty things. Once discovered in the 1800's, steam became a powerful resource for moving people and commodities around the country with locomotives. It's also true in your extra one degree pursuit of excellence in music ministry.

In Olympic ski racing the margin of victory of the men's giant slalom competition has been a mere 0.17 seconds. The extra effort won the gold medal. It is said that the average margin of victory in the last twenty five years of major gold tournaments combined has been less than three strokes. Indy 500 car racing reports the average margin of

---

[36]Scripture reference — John 17:20

victory over the last ten years has been 1.54 seconds. That little extra effort made the difference.

Grab your Bible, pray in the Holy Ghost, stir your enthusiasm and passion for souls, and refuse to be lazy with your gifts. Demand excellence of yourself. Once you stretch in this regard, you'll never again accept mediocrity.

Here's my last suggestion or rather my last direction. If it's needed, just get back on the hillside with some of them sheep. Stay a while and sing, sing, sing—play, play, play, of course, this time in tune with excellence. I believe your future is so bright you'll have to buy a new pair of shades to wear indoors.

EPILOGUE

It has been a delight for me to spend this time with you, my new friend. I am honored and blessed and sincerely trust that we'll share more times together. Hopefully, you have acquired some valuable information that will change your daily habits in a positive way. It certainly is obtainable and the rewards are spectacular. When we all arrive at our next place of eternal ministry, we'll look back and marvel at how easy it really was. The Father God has had our back the whole time, prodding, urging the Holy Spirit to inform us of details.

I encourage you to utilize all the tools that God gives us today, especially in regard to technology. The Internet, or WWW path, is the new roman road, a metaphor for the spreading of the Gospel. In the Apostle Paul's day of evangelism and building churches, he travelled down every available road with the Gospel. He didn't have to invent those roads, maintain them, or invest in them. They were already there. Use every available voice; radio, TV, internet, podcast, YouTube, Facebook, Twitter, and whatever else will come. Get your iPods, iPads, notebooks and mp3's happin'! Use all the tools and do it with musical and spiritual excellence.

Of late, I've noted with concern that there is a lack of musical and spiritual truth in some material that has become popularized in church circles. My effort in mentioning even a whisper concerning this is not censorship but rather as concern. It is to underscore again that excellence is found in the details. A goofy, religious sounding lyric or sloppy musicianship in constructing songs is immature, superficial, and frankly is dis-honoring of our Savior. The world sees right through it.

Don't try to mix sound Biblical truth with human psychology. Lyrics of doubt and unbelief should not be found in your composition. If it takes special lights, tunings and weird looks to sell the song, then maybe you should re-think it or better yet re-write it. Stay with the Word and do what you do with excellence. I understand that my roots of rock-n-roll, jazz and some formal classical training, may be a filter of a sort, but I speak with some experience as to watching trends and styles.

The language of music is a spiritual vernacular and the older you grow, you hear it and see it even better, recognizing the anointing when it's present. One example comes to mind. Cheryl and I were ministering in Birmingham, England in a crusade. We scheduled a few extra days of R&R and were invited to come to Bristol for a Sunday afternoon meeting at a small church. We arrived early (you're never on time unless you're early) and met with the pastor. Since we were to minister in song and teaching, I asked to meet the music director. He said "Well, that's my wife and daughter and they're in the sanctuary now, rehearsing." "Good, let's go and meet them," I said. Upon going into the auditorium, I heard two nice female voices accompanied by an un-tuned acoustic guitar and accordion. Hum, I thought and chuckled to myself, "Lawrence Welk praise and worship?" [37] What? No real sound system? No digital keyboard? No hip groove drummer? My sad American musical elitist attitude was soon removed and buried as praise and worship unfolded that afternoon. Their anointed music resulted in an awesome move of God, which manifested long before we sang or played a note. These precious two vessels of honor, a mother and daughter, were obviously in love with Jesus. I repented and I was blessed.

Another experience was in Soweto, South Africa. We were involved at a leadership conference held at Rhema Bible Church in Johannesburg, hosted by Tom Inglis' School of Psalmody. Richard Roberts and many other wonderful speakers were there. We accompanied an Australian pastor friend, Tony Fitzgerald who has pioneered churches in many nations, to a small mission in the South African ghetto of Soweto. At this time, the awful apartheid attitude and law was still in effect, but

---

[37] 2011, en.wikepedia.org/wikipedia/lawrencewelk

we were on a mission and have always been color blind. We had taken a wonderfully talented saxophonist from Niagara Falls, Chu Nero, with us as well. We traveled down dirt roads and finally entered a small shanty that was grossly overcrowded with people. It was a standing room only crowd. Inside we found a dirt floor and only a single light bulb in the middle of the room. Someone had brought a generator so I could have electricity for my keyboard and Cheryl's microphone. It was amazing to experience such intense worship.

Do you know what "chuch" is? We had *real* church that night. The anointing in the music drew an even bigger crowd. Then as Pastor Tony ministered, we saw miracle after miracle take place. Our interpreter was translating in three different languages every other sentence, so that everyone would understand some of the message. Again, we gave it our best in music, passion, energy, and love. We were required finally to leave, but rejoiced because God showed up so mightily that evening.

Growing up in the rural South Georgia city of Bainbridge, I had no idea that one quality decision to receive Jesus and follow Him would eventually take me around the world in ministry. I've had the privilege of playing one of the world's finest Hamburg Steinway pianos at the Sydney Opera House in Australia. Cheryl and I have done concerts and music ministry on the moon like terrain of Reykjavík, Iceland on an air force base. We've ministered around the world, and there are still galaxies beyond.

My last thought may need some theological conjecturing. I believe that God has an awesome continuous plan unfolding as we approach moving to Heaven and participating in Heaven's tasks. I'm sure that light, Love, and sound are enormous there, and I suggest that as psalmists and leaders, we'll have a lot of ministering to do and even more songs to write when we get there. Heaven is a real place and we'll be employed there. I don't think that the ministry of healing or evangelism will be as needed in Heaven. Guess what? That means job security! We musicians/singers/psalmists should be equipped to be vessels of honor, sanctified, especially useful to the Master, and prepared to do every good work with excellence.

ABOUT THE AUTHOR

The ministry of Steve Ingram encompasses over forty years of teaching, preaching, and music ministry. From his days as director of the pioneering contemporary Christian band, Alpenglow, sponsored by the Christian Broadcasting Network's Housetop Records and directing the music for Kenneth Copeland Ministries, he has learned practical and spiritual aspects of flowing in the anointing of the Holy Spirit. The IMI School of Ministry and Music was birthed out of Steve and Cheryl Ingram's Schools of the Psalmist conducted worldwide.

Steve is known for teaching spiritual and musical excellence. Thousands of musicians and singers have benefited from his word and faith based teaching ministry. He is an accomplished musician. While his technique and touch on the acoustic piano have put him in demand as an accompanist, his expertise with the keyboard and digital technology places him in a unique group of knowledgeable Gospel players. Steve has the special ability to flow musically with the Spirit of God. His use of sounds and colors on the keyboards paints musical pictures of what is happening in the concert or service.

He has attended Florida State University, Valdosta State College and holds an Associate of Arts Degree from North Florida Junior College and an Honorary Doctorate of Sacred Music from Life Christian University.

Steve has released an instrumental, Biblical, meditation trilogy called, *Sounds of Love, Sounds of Joy* and *Sounds of Peace*. The project consists of scriptures, which Steve interprets musically. The result is beautiful music that is moving, uplifting, and soothing. He is a member of ASCAP, the American Society of Composers, Authors and Publishers.

Dr. Steve Ingram is the Founding Senior Pastor of Word of Faith Family Church located in Orlando Florida. (Altamonte Springs) He and his wife lead a vibrant church team who are teaching people how to "live Victoriously by Faith in Jesus Christ and actively participate in the world-wide harvest of souls." They have one son, Steve Jr. www.woffc.tv

RECOMMENDED RESOURCES

These are wonderful days of readily available information and resources for learning as never before. The internet has opened a very wide door to seeing various levels of people doing wonderful exploits for the Kingdom of God. The internet has also increased accessibility, enabling anyone to see lyrics, and guitar chords for many worship songs, and download MP3-MP4 tracks. This has also played a part in the globalization of much contemporary worship. Some churches, such as Hillsong and Vineyard, have their own publishing companies, and there is a thriving Christian music business which parallels that of the secular world, with recording studios, music books, CDs, MP3-MP4 tracks downloads and other merchandise.

The web addresses found here may have changed due to the rapid growth of the internet. This list is given without bias or preference and is certainly not exhaustive. Here are a few to consider.

PraiseCharts.com-Thousands of worship leaders and musicians from all around the world have discovered a gold mine of resources at Praise Charts, ready to download, print and play. Everything is at your fingertips, just a few clicks away. www.praisecharts.com

WorshipIdeas.com-This web site has free music and practical ideas for today's contemporary praise and worship services. They give wonderful aids for modulations, top ten lists and insights to everything under the heading of worship. www.worshipideas.com

Church Production Magazine-This is a monthly magazine that focuses on audio, video, lighting and the technological aspects of houses of worship. www.churchproduction.com

Steve Bowersox- Bowersox Institute of Music- University of Mobile, Chair of Worship. Psalmist, worship leader, and clinician. His leadership and teaching style is always filled with encouragement for all. Steve has many excellent resources for Music Theory, Vocal Aerobics and more. www.bowersoxinstitute.com

Angela Courte Ministries-Orlando, Florida; singer, teacher, TV Host of the Power of Praise, a nationally syndicated television program that includes new songs and generally one hymn per week and its story. She is an excellent resource for women in ministry. www.AngelaCourte.com

Ben Tankard Ministry-Nashville, Tennessee; a highly skilled pianist and producer and has been recording professionally since 1990. His fluid keyboard style is mellow and inspirational, peppered with a gospel jazz anointing. www.bentankardministries.com

Life Christian University-Tampa, Florida; wonderful resource for continuing education from seasoned Spirit-filled instructors with various online international campuses, as well as the Tampa, Florida main campus (Dr. Doug Wingate President). www.president@lcu.edu

Len Mink Ministries- Tulsa, Oklahoma; a gifted psalmist and composer-songwriter of many worship projects. He has worked for nearly 40 years as the worshiper for Kenneth Copeland meetings world-wide. Len and Cathy have their own daily television program on the TCT television network seen in 173 countries, and on DIRECTV channel 377 and the Time Warner network. www.LenMink.com

Mighty Horn Ministries-Phil Driscoll is a world class trumpet player/ singer/ composer and a consummate performer whose Grammy-winning music draws strength from his dynamic personality and passion for God. www.contact@mightyhorn.com

Morris Chapman Ministries-Las Vegas, Nevada; songwriter, worship leader, and minister. Morris is known around the world for his ability to lead people into the presence of the Lord. He began full time ministry in 1978 and his songs are widely recognized around the world, especially in praise and worship. www.info@morrischapman.org

Bethel Music is an American worship group from Redding, California, where they started making music in 2001, at Bethel Church. Great resource of worship. www.Bethelmusic.com

Kenneth Copeland Bible College - KCBC Ft. Worth, Texas. The Mission of Kenneth Copeland Bible College is to serve as a world-class institution of Biblical higher education, providing skillful Word-of-Faith based instruction with integrity and excellence. www.kcbiblecollege.org KCBC P.O. Box 475, Newark, TX 76071 info@kcbiblecollege.org